# WILD ORCHIDS OF TEXAS

NUMBER FORTY-TWO *The Corrie Herring Hooks Series*

# WILD ORCHIDS OF TEXAS

BY *Joe Liggio* AND *Ann Orto Liggio*

PHOTOGRAPHS BY *Joe Liggio*

SCIENTIFIC ADVISOR *David H. Riskind*

*University of Texas Press*    AUSTIN

"From Blazes to Blooms" originally appeared in a slightly different form in the January 1991 issue of *Texas Parks & Wildlife* magazine.

Designed by Ellen McKie

LIBRARY OF CONGRESS CATALOGING-IN-PUBLICATION DATA

Liggio, Joe.
   Wild orchids of Texas / by Joe Liggio and Ann Liggio ; photographs by Joe Liggio ; scientific advisor, David H. Riskind. — 1st ed.
        p.    cm. — (The Corrie Herring Hooks series ; no. 42)
   Includes bibliographical references (p.    ) and index.
   ISBN 0-292-74712-8 (cloth : alk. paper)
   1. Orchids—Texas—Identification.  2. Orchids—Texas—Pictorial works.  I. Liggio, Ann.  II. Title.  III. Series.
QK495.O64L539    1999
584'.4'09764—dc21                                                        98-51720

# Contents

# PREFACE

$\mathcal{N}$early five thousand species of vascular plants have been catalogued in Texas, a large number that reflects the diverse climate and topography of the Lone Star State. Many books and articles for the layperson and professional botanist alike have been devoted to the flora of Texas, but until now, no regional guide to the orchids of Texas has existed. In writing this book, we want first and foremost to share the beauty of these exquisite orchids of Texas. We also want to provide a guide with the most recent information with regard to taxonomy and distribution of orchids in Texas. To achieve both these ends, we have included a liberal number of color photographs, images that we hope will give pleasure and allow even the weekend naturalist to identify these wild orchids and become alert to their typical habitats.

Regional guides to wild orchids, such as those listed in the bibliography, yielded valuable information, but our work would have taken longer without Donovan Correll's monumental works, *Flora of Texas, Orchidaceae* (1944) and *Native Orchids of North America* (1950), and Carlyle Luer's *Native Orchids of Florida* (1972) and *Native Orchids of the United States and Canada* (1975). We consulted many regional guides to wild orchids; two that were especially helpful to our research on ecology and habitats were *Orchids of the Western Great Lakes Region* (1987) by Frederick W. Case, Jr., and *An Introduction to the Ecology of the Illinois Orchidaceae* (1974) by Charles Sheviak.

We visited several major university herbariums in Texas to gather information about locations and bloom times. In this project, we are greatly indebted to our friend David Berkshire of Houston, both for his research assistance at the herbariums and for his computer expertise in assembling and analyzing the data.

Except where otherwise noted, all photographs in this book were taken by Joe Liggio. Beginning in 1979, he spent hundreds of hours in the Big Thicket of East Texas and made dozens of trips to the mountains of Trans-Pecos Texas and Big Bend National Park to find and photograph sometimes elusive species of wild orchids. Our descriptions of orchids and their habitats incorporate much of his direct observations in the field.

# Acknowledgments

We are deeply grateful for the help and support of many individuals and organizations. Meeting people who share the same enthusiasm for delicate flowers was as much a pleasure as finding a rare orchid for the first time. Our greatest thanks must go to our longtime friend David C. Berkshire, who reviewed many drafts of our manuscript and offered valuable suggestions. He also donated many hours of his time to create the range maps based on information we supplied. His help extended to the field, as he accompanied us on countless treks over rough terrain on some of the hottest days a Texas summer can produce.

We also wish to thank Shannon Davies, our sponsoring editor at UT Press, who always believed in this book; David H. Riskind, our scientific advisor, for his insight and constructive criticism; Steve Orzell, who provided much information and literature on the distribution and ecology of Texas orchids; and John and Gloria Tveten, who first encouraged us to write about Texas orchids.

Others who helped by offering suggestions, accompanying us on field trips, or directing us to elusive orchids include Susan and Van Metzler, Larry E. Brown, Jeff Schultz, David Snell, Frank Gregg, Geraldine Watson, Tom Todsen, William R. Carr, Tom and Betty Alex, Mike Fleming, Jackie Poole, Kathy Parker, Hugh Wilson, Nelwyn McInnis, Michael and Barbara MacRoberts, Will McDearman, Lawrence K. Magrath, Bruce and Lana Ewing, Osa Hall, Osa Hall, Jr., Claude A. McLeod, Victor S. Engel, Douglas H. Goldman, Ted

Hollingsworth, Kelly Bryant, Mark Lockwood, Angus Gholson, Wilson Baker, Jean Hardy, Howard Peacock, Leila Merritt, Barton Warnock, Carl R. Slaughter, Carl G. Hunter, Nancy E. Cowden, Suzanne Walker, Brett Wauer, and Fred Armstrong.

Curators and professional staff members of many herbariums in Texas helped us research the distribution of orchid species, both by providing access to herbarium collections and by sending herbarium specimens or records. Those who were especially helpful include A. Michael Powell, Sul Ross State University; Stephan L. Hatch, Texas A&M University; Elray S. Nixon, Stephen F. Austin State University; Guy Nesom and Tom Wendt, University of Texas; Barney L. Lipscomb, Botanical Research Institute of Texas (BRIT); Bonnie B. Amos, Angelo State University; Richard Worthington, University of Texas at El Paso; W. C. Holmes, Baylor University; Tony Keeney, Southwest Texas Junior College; and Arthur M. Elliot, Texas Tech University. We also received helpful information from Charles J. Sheviak, New York State Museum, and A. A. Reznicek, University of Michigan.

# WILD ORCHIDS OF TEXAS

# $\mathscr{T}$EXAS TREASURES

*Confucius called the
orchid the "king of
fragrant plants."*

$\mathscr{W}$orldwide, approximately twenty-five thousand species of wild orchids are known to botanists. A total of fifty-four types of wild orchids grow within the 267,000 square miles of Texas. This includes fifty-two species and two varieties. Admittedly, fifty-four is a modest number compared to the number of species found in Costa Rica, where twelve hundred orchid species can be found in 19,000 square miles. The common notion of orchids is that they grow only in tropical climates such as that of Costa Rica, so it may surprise some readers to learn that wild orchids grow throughout North America, even north of the Arctic Circle. In fact, the state flower of Minnesota is the pink-and-white Lady's slipper orchid *(Cypripedium reginae),* also called the showy Lady's slipper orchid.

One reason Texas has a respectable number of orchid species is that its diverse climate and topography create ideal conditions for orchids that are native to the eastern United States, the southwestern United States, and Mexico. A vast coastal plain that begins around New Jersey on the Atlantic Coast stretches south to Florida. Extending westward along the Gulf Coast into Texas, this coastal plain is covered with rich pine and hardwood forests dotted with swamps, ponds, bogs, savannahs, seepage springs, and meadows, creating a mosaic of habitats that support a large variety of orchids. Many orchid species found along this coastal plain reach their western range limit in Texas.

Although the greatest number of orchid species in Texas—about thirty-six—inhabit the moist forests of

East Texas, many species flourish in the moist canyons of the Edwards Plateau and the mountains of Trans-Pecos Texas (Amerson et al. 1975). As you move west and south across Texas, the average annual rainfall diminishes, from nearly 60 inches near the Sabine River in East Texas to less than 8 inches at El Paso in far West Texas. As you move south, annual rainfall drops to about 20 inches in Brownsville. The number of orchid species declines accordingly. Few orchids of the eastern United States reach beyond the Balcones Escarpment of the Edwards Plateau in Central Texas. Most orchids found on the Edwards Plateau are primarily species of the southwestern United States, Chihuahuan Desert, and Mexican Sierra Madre. In arid Trans-Pecos Texas, high mountains give orchids refuge from the desert in cool, damp forests, wooded ravines, and canyons.

Orchids in Texas range from the High Plains of the Panhandle down to the *resacas* (oxbow lakes) of the lower Rio Grande Valley along the Mexican border. Orchids that grow in the wilds of Texas prefer temperate climates. Although temperate orchids are generally much smaller and less conspicuous than their tropical cousins, their delicate beauty is still worthy of the name "orchid."

Unlike tropical orchids, the vast majority of native North American orchids, including all those native to Texas, are terrestrial, growing with their roots firmly embedded in soil. North America does have a few species of epiphytic, or tree-dwelling orchids, but for the most part they are restricted to tropical Florida. (Of the terrestrial orchids, scientists know of two species that grow totally underground: *Rhizanthella gardneri* and *Cryptanthemis slateri,* both in Australia.)

## VANISHING HABITATS

Loss of habitat is by far the greatest threat to orchids and other rare plants in Texas. When Texas was a vast, mostly unpopulated wilderness, many orchids were undoubtedly much more common. Today, much of this original wilderness has been altered by farming, ranching, industry, and residential development, so many orchid habitats have disappeared. Some orchid species that are adapted to special environments, such as the southern Lady's slipper *(Cypripedium kentuckiense)*, have all but vanished along with their habitats. However, a few weedy orchids, such as spring ladies tresses *(Spiranthes vernalis)* and the nodding ladies tresses *(S. cernua)*, can adapt to a wide range of habitats and may be more common today than they were in the past.

Although many famous orchid haunts visited by botanists in the past are now gone, a surprising number of good orchid habitats remain in Texas—not by accident, but as the result of efforts of a multitude of dedicated Texans. For many years, Texas conservationists have worked to save such treasures as Big Bend National Park, Guadalupe Mountains National Park, the Big Thicket National Preserve, and East Texas wilderness areas in the national forests. Also, the U.S. Forest Service maintains many special habitats in the Texas national forests as botanical areas, scenic areas, and research natural areas. In these areas, a variety of rare, delicate wildflowers and orchids thrive. Many state parks and wildlife management areas administered by Texas Parks & Wildlife Department also preserve important orchid habitats. Still other orchid habitats are protected by The Nature Conservancy and other private conservation organizations. Unfortunately, important habitats for several rare orchids, including the snowy orchid *(Platanthera nivea)*, Chapman's orchid *(P. chapmanii)*, the crested fringed orchid *(P. cristata)*, and the giant spiral orchid *(Spiranthes longilabris)*, remain underrepresented in preserves today. Without protection, these orchids, along with their habitats, may soon vanish from the Texas landscape.

## CARELESS COLLECTORS

Another threat to our native orchids comes from a surprising source: orchid enthusiasts. Regrettably, some people dig up wild orchids and remove them from their natural habitats, even though most species of wild orchids are almost impossible to transplant successfully (Luer 1972, Koopowitz and Kaye 1983, Homoya 1993,

*. . . it must be
stressed that the
native orchids we
now possess should
not be "collected";
and that an . . .
enthusiast should
think of himself as
an orchid observer,
exactly as a "bird
watcher" is not a
bird collector. The
great majority of
native orchids are
so sensitive in their
delicate balance
with their environ-
ment that they
cannot hope to
survive transplant-
ing. To collect one is
comparable to the
trapping of a wild
bird by a bird
watcher. Uncom-
mon species could
be quickly extermi-
nated, as many
have been. How
much more would
have been gained by
field trips to gather
pertinent data
on variations,
situations, seasons,
and weather, than
by stealing plants
eventually doomed
to perish in pot or
garden.*

CARLYLE LUER

Smith 1993). Nearly every forest ranger or nature guide has one or more stories about pointing out an extremely endangered plant to a visiting garden club or similar group, only to come upon members of the very same group digging the plant up the next day.

Some may believe they cause no harm to native orchid species when they buy them from commercial growers. Native orchids are offered by some commercial nurseries with the assurances that none have been collected from the wild. However, many times, wild-collected plants that remain in a nursery for only one growing season are then sold under claims of being "nursery grown" (a practice called "nursery-laundering").

Threats to wild orchids do not come just from orchid hobbyists and commercial growers. Unenlightened botanists who collect specimens for herbariums can also contribute to the decline of rare orchid species. Although it is important to document new locations for rare species, all unnecessary collecting should be avoided, especially when only a few individual plants are found. Although collecting has little adverse effect on common orchid species, it can have a devastating effect on species already in peril. Alternatives to collecting, for purposes of scientific documentation, include photographs, sketches, measurements, and detailed notes.

In the foreword to *Field Guide to Orchids of North America* (Williams and Williams 1983), Roger Tory Peterson argues, "In today's world few orchids can afford the attrition imposed by the vasculum [carrying case] and the plant press."

## THE FUTURE OF ORCHIDS IN TEXAS

The only way to ensure the future survival of wild orchids is to preserve their habitats. Many areas in Texas have already been set aside for national and state parks, wilderness areas, and wildlife refuges. These areas will require careful management and continued stewardship to ensure preservation of orchids and other wild plants. Although such places contribute greatly to the preservation of many species, we still need additional parks and preserves if we are to succeed in saving several of our more rare and threatened orchids and wildflowers.

In some of the most significant conservation work in recent years, the Endangered Resource Branch of the Texas Parks & Wildlife Department has worked closely with The Texas Nature Conservancy to identify habitats that need to be preserved. The Texas Nature Conservancy—a private, nonprofit organization funded by contributions from individuals, foundations, and corporations—tries to purchase sites that are home to endangered or threatened species. Government and industry can also help preserve habitats through creative management of easements and rights-of-way associated with highways, railroads, pipelines, and power lines. Such management would include conducting extensive botanical surveys, mowing at proper times (which can actually benefit many sun-loving orchids), and eliminating use of herbicides. A cooperative effort between conservationists, governments, and private business will go far toward preserving our wild orchids.

We also need more legal protection for our priceless native orchids and other rare wildflowers. Today, the only wild orchid in Texas that is specifically protected by law is the Navasota ladies tresses orchid, declared an endangered species in 1982.

## How to Save Our Native Orchids: What You Can Do

- Contribute money and time to environmental and conservation groups working to protect and conserve wild orchids and other rare plants.
- When hiking in a park or nature preserve, stay on the trail. Disturbing the soil around an orchid can kill it. Wetland pine savannahs and hillside seepage bogs are especially fragile, and hikers can easily damage the delicate plants that thrive there.
- Photographing wild orchids can also be harmful to them, so be careful when taking pictures. Do not remove fading blossoms that contain developing seeds.
- Never pick, cut, or dig up any rare plants in the wild. Leave them where you find them.
- If you see someone "collecting" a wild plant in a state or national park, speak up! The "collector" may be unaware that this activity can wipe out entire species, and may also not realize that collecting plants is illegal in state and national parks, as well as on Texas state highway roadsides.
- If persuasion doesn't work, report the poacher to the park or forest ranger. Try to get the poacher's car license number.

*Although mention of the word "orchid" usually brings to mind sweltering jungles in far-off lands, shrouded in mystery and romance, such need not be the case, for perhaps the small patch of woodland lying within a stone's throw of one's home may harbor several species of these much sought-after plants.*

DONOVAN S. CORRELL

*The beauty of woodland wild-flowers is that they exist at all. Finding a painted trillium or a pink lady's slipper elicits exclamations of admiration, as much from surprise that such a delicate flower is thriving unattended as from an appreciation of its form or color.*

ROGER B. SWAIN

# *A*N INFINITE VARIETY

*A*ll living organisms are classified by kingdom, phylum, class, order, family, genus, and species, based on biological and anatomical similarities. Orchids are members of the class of plants called the angiosperms (Angiospermae), the flowering plants. The angiosperms are divided into two subclasses: the monocots (Monocotyledonae) and the dicots (Dicotyledonae). This division is based on the number of cotyledons (embryonic seed leaves) contained within the seed. The seeds of monocots usually contain one cotyledon, while the seeds of dicots contain two. Orchids are classified as monocots, although their tiny seeds do not contain a cotyledon like that of a typical monocot. All orchids are members of the family Orchidaceae.

## SLIPPERS, SPIDERS, AND SNAKES
### *A Spectacular Spectrum of Shapes*

Members of the orchid family come in a myriad of sizes—from flowers tinier than the head of a straight pin *(Platystele ornata)* to blooms with spurs more than a foot long *(Angraecum sesquipidale).* The various shapes of orchids have been compared with violins, dragonflies, buckets, shoes, ducks, scorpions, and snake mouths, to name a few. This variety reflects the countless ways orchids have evolved to accommodate a multitude of different pollinators.

Although orchids display a marvelous array of flower forms, they all share several basic features that mark them as members of the orchid family. Most orchid

The spiral, a fundamental form in nature, is splendidly illustrated in *Spiranthes* orchids.

The pouchlike lip of *Cypripedium* forms an intricate trap that forces escaping bees into pollinating its flower.

In the typical orchid, the lip is the lowermost part of the flower, but in *Calopogon* orchids the lip is uppermost.

*Platanthera ciliaris* has an intricately fringing lip, a common feature of the *Platanthera* genus.

*Hexalectris warnockii*, like other members of *Hexalectris* genus, has a lip marked by several wavy crests.

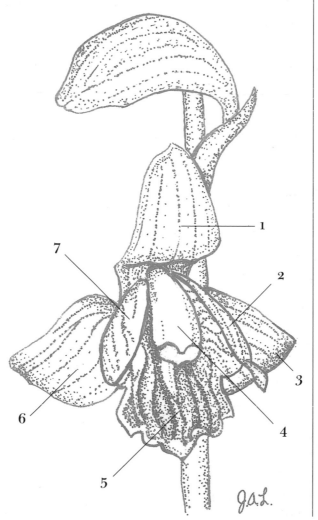

flowers consist of an outer whorl made up of three sepals, and an inner whorl made up of three petals. One of the petals, the lip, is strikingly different from the other two. Sometimes these structures can be fused or reduced. In orchids, the male and the female flower parts are not completely separated, but are fused into a single club-shaped form known as the column, which projects from the center of the flower. Except for the genus *Cypripedium,* which has two anthers, most North American orchids have a single anther, located near the top of the column. The anther contains pollen usually grouped into small masses called *pollinia.* The female stigma, a sticky, depressed surface that receives the pollinia, is directly below the anther. The ovary, which contains

*The contrivances by which orchids are fertilised are as varied and almost as perfect as any of the most beautiful adaptations in the animal kingdom.*

CHARLES DARWIN
(1877)

FIGURE 1
Parts of an orchid

1. Sepal

2. Petal

3. Sepal

4. Column

5. Lip

6. Sepal

7. Petal

the female egg cells (ovules), is underneath the stigma. After fertilization occurs, the ovary containing the developing seeds swells and forms the seed capsule. On the column, a downward-projecting structure called the *rostellum* separates the anther from the stigma and prevents self-pollination in cross-pollinating orchids. The rostellum also provides a sticky glue that aids in the transfer of pollen to the pollinator.

Because of the way orchid flower structure has evolved, each orchid species is pollinated by a specific

*Hexalectris spicata*
var. *spicata*
crested coral root

type of animal pollinator. This highly evolved characteristic inhibits hybridization between different orchid species, thus ensuring the integrity of each species. This has also led to the evolution of many different species. The elaborate pollination mechanisms of orchids result in large amounts of pollen being transferred between flowers so that fewer visits by pollinators (such as insects) are necessary to ensure fertilization and high seed production.

## POLLINATION BY INSECTS

What accounts for the fantastic variety in the orchid family? Why do orchids have such a huge variety of sizes, shapes, colors, and scents? Because orchids rely on animals and insects for pollination, they must advertise and they usually offer rewards. Different colors and flower forms are adapted to distinct types of pollinators. Some orchids attract pollinators by appearance, while others attract by means of scent.

The gaudy colors and strange forms displayed by many orchid species are designed to lure pollinators and accommodate their visits. Most orchids even provide landing platforms for pollinators in the form of the lip, which is the lowest part of the flower in most species. It is usually brightly colored to attract pollinators, and as a further enticement, may be adorned with stripes, spots, or crests; it may also be fluted, rolled, or "bearded" along the edge. Often, the lip is structured so that it can guide the pollinator into precisely the right position to assure pollination.

Not all orchids display the lip in the lower position. For example, the grass pink and Oklahoma grass pink (*Calopogon* spp.), the snowy orchid *(Platanthera nivea)*, and the shadow witch *(Ponthieva racemosa)* all hold their lips uppermost. As the orchid bud opens, the pedicel (the stem supporting individual flowers), gradually twists 180 degrees, positioning the lip in the lower position, the usual position for most orchids. This twisting process is called *resupination.*

In typical insect pollination, an insect enters a flower and pushes its way under the column to drink the nectar. As the insect withdraws, pollen that has stuck to its body during a previous visit to another orchid rubs off on the stigma of this orchid. Withdrawing farther, the insect presses against the rostellum, a structure that separates the anther from the stigma and provides a sticky "glue." When the insect, now coated with this sticky substance, brushes against the anther, it picks up pollen. The pollen sticks to the insect in the precise spot where it will touch the stigma of the next flower.

As examples of this type of pollination, consider the members of the genus *Platanthera.* These orchids bear nectar-containing spurs that descend from the base of the lip. The yellow fringed orchid *(P. ciliaris),* with a spur more than 1 inch long, is pollinated by the swallowtail butterfly, which has a long proboscis—a straw-like mouthpiece for sucking. The anther of this *Platanthera* orchid is positioned so that pollen attaches to the compound eyes on each side of the butterfly's proboscis as it sips nectar (Folsom 1984). When the butterfly visits another yellow fringed orchid, pollen is deposited on the stigma of the second orchid, completing pollination.

Some orchids do not offer nectar or any other reward, but deceive a potential pollinator by their resemblance to other flowers that do. An example of this is the grass pink, a member of the genus *Calopogon.*

Orchids may attract not only by appearance, but also by scent. The fragrant ladies tresses *(Spiranthes odorata),* for example, has a sweet aroma mindful of vanilla and jasmine. Some orchids have such peculiar scents that they may even smell offensive to humans. One strange example from the Mediterranean region is the Ophyrs orchid *(Ophyrs speculum),* which attracts the male wasp by looking and smelling like a female wasp.

## SELF-POLLINATION IN ORCHIDS

In a family that has evolved elaborate mechanisms to ensure cross-pollination, self-pollination in orchids is an astonishing occurrence; but in several orchid genera, including the *Corallorhiza, Hexalectris,* and *Platanthera,* self-pollination is common. For orchids colonizing new territory where pollinators are scarce or nonexistent, self-pollination offers a significant advantage (Catling and Catling 1991), because it allows these orchids to produce generations of offspring without the aid of an animal pollinator. At least four Texas orchids are known for self-pollination: the autumn coral root *(Corallorhiza odontorhiza),* the Glass Mountain coral root *(Hexalectris nitida),* the Arizona crested coral root *(H. spicata* var. *arizonica),* and the little club-spur orchid *(Platanthera clavellata).* Flowers of self-pollinating orchids are often smaller and less attractive than those of cross-pollinating orchids of the same species, and sometimes the flowers never open. Self-pollinating flowers that remain closed are referred to as cleistogamous, Latin for "closed union."

## Vegetative Seed Production *(Apomixis)*

Other orchid genera have in some instances forsaken pollination altogether. Seeds are developed without pollination through a process called *apomixis,* a Greek term meaning "away from mixing." This refers to seed production without mixing or fusion of sex cells in pollination. In this process, seeds are produced vegetatively from tissue surrounding the ovule (the female sex cell contained in the ovary). Like self-pollination, apomixis offers a critical advantage to orchids that inhabit regions where pollinators are scarce or absent (Catling and Catling 1991). Embryos contained within seeds produced by apomixis are clones that are genetically identical to the seed-producing mother plant. This form of seed production is prevalent in the *Spiranthes* genus, especially in *S. cernua.* Apomixis is the only known mode of seed production in the Navasota ladies tresses *(S. parksii).* As in self-pollinating orchids, apomictic orchids are usually smaller, are less showy, and sometimes have closed flowers.

## Saprophytic Orchids

Perhaps the strangest of our native orchids are the saprophytes. Saprophytic plants derive their nutrients primarily from decaying leaves and vegetable matter. Texas has nine species of saprophytic orchids, four in the genus *Corallorhiza* and five in the genus *Hexalectris*. Saprophytic orchids can be among the most difficult to find; although many are richly decorated with bright, exotic colors like ornate candy sticks, they often grow in deep shade and bloom for only a short time. In addition, most of their life span is spent underground as branching, coral-like rhizomes. (A rhizome is an underground stem that functions much like a root.) They are the most ephemeral of all orchids, usually appearing just long enough to erect a naked, leafless flower stalk, bloom, and produce seed capsules, with the entire sequence lasting perhaps only a few weeks.

Saprophytic orchids contain very little chlorophyll, and usually have no green color at all in the entire plant. Some authors refer to flowering saprophytic plants as *mycotrophic,* which literally means "living on fungi." Saprophytic orchids cannot digest leaf litter and rotting wood without the aid of a symbiotic fungus. The fungus provides starches, sugars, and other important nutrients.

# THE
# DISCRIMINATING
# ORCHID

ompared to many other types of plants, orchids are relatively rare. Often, their very existence is precarious, requiring exacting conditions related to seed placement, soil, sunlight and shade, and periodic disturbance of the habitat. The requirements of orchids sometimes seem peculiar: for example, bog orchids such as the rose pogonia *(Pogonia ophioglossoides)*, the grass pink *(Calopogon tuberosus)*, the yellow fringed orchid *(Platanthera ciliaris)*, and the snowy orchid *(P. nivea)* grow in sterile soil where there is plenty of sunlight and water. The soil they prefer lacks so many vital nutrients that it is unsuitable for most plants. Although forest-dwelling orchids often grow in the shade in humus-rich forests, it is essential that they emerge in late winter or early spring before the forest canopy has leafed out. During this brief sunny period, the woodland orchids photosynthesize, store nutrients, and bloom.

Not all orchid species are particular about their habitats. Some species of ladies tresses, such as *Spiranthes vernalis, S. cernua, S. praecox,* and *S. lacera* var. *gracilis,* are common because they can flourish in a wide range of conditions. They often thrive in sites that have been heavily disturbed by human activities; these sites include roadsides, abandoned farmland, vacant lots, and even manicured lawns.

## Seeds: *Risky Business*

In the life cycle of an orchid, much is left to chance. This may explain why many orchids are rare even though they produce an incredibly large number of seeds. Because most orchid species have exacting habitat requirements, only a few of their many seeds are likely to land in a suitable environment. As an indication of how demanding an orchid species can be, most require that a suitable mycorrhizal fungus be present in the soil. Adding to the tenuous situation, most orchid seeds remain viable for only a few weeks. Even if an orchid seed lands in an ideal spot at an ideal time and sprouts, it may take several years to mature, bloom, and produce seeds of its own—at which time the precarious cycle begins anew.

## The Orchid-Fungus Partnership
### *Mycorrhiza*

A critical development in the life history of an orchid is the establishment of a mycorrhizal relationship with a symbiotic fungus. The word *mycorrhiza* is derived from two Greek words that mean "fungus" and "root," and alludes to a symbiotic relationship, the biological association between a fungus and the underground parts of an orchid plant. This mycorrhizal relationship begins with the germination of the orchid seed. Unlike the seeds of most flowering plants, an orchid seed lacks the endosperm, a layer of cells that furnishes food for developing seedlings. Without its own source of food, the orchid seed requires an associated mycorrhizal fungus to provide the necessary nutrients for seedling development.

Mycorrhizal associations between orchids and their fungal partners are not highly specific, and orchids are apparently able to form symbiotic relationships with a variety of saprophytic and parasitic soil fungi (Harley and Smith 1983).

The vegetative part of a mycorrhizal fungus found in the soil is called a *mycelium*. This fungal mycelium is made up of hundreds of tiny threadlike strands of cells called *hyphae* that form an extensive branching network throughout a large area of soil. The part of a mycorrhizal fungus that forms an interface with the tissue inside the orchid seed represents only a small portion of the fungal mycelium. The extensive network of hyphae of the fungal partner serves as a greatly expanded root system for the developing orchid seedling, allowing the orchid extraordinary access to soil nutrients (Doherty 1997). The orchid obtains a variety of substances from its mycorrhizal fungus, including water, nitrogen, phosphorous, mineral salts, carbohydrates, and other organic compounds (Rasmussen 1995).

If an orchid seed lands where environmental conditions are suitable for germination, early stages of growth may begin, but without the aid of a mycorrhizal fungus, the seedling will not develop any further. When an orchid seed lands in a favorable spot and forms an association with a compatible fungus in the soil, seedling development can proceed. Successful germination begins with the penetration of the orchid seed by its mycorrhizal fungus. When the hyphae of this fungus penetrate the orchid embryo through a tiny pore in the seed coat, the orchid responds by releasing chemical substances that control the fungal infection by confining it to specialized cells within the orchid seed. Within these cells, the fungal hyphae form dense coils or clumps of nutrient-rich material. These clumps are then digested by the orchid to furnish the needed nutrients for seedling development (Dressler 1981).

With time, the orchid embryo develops into a protocorm, a mass of cells shaped like a toy spinning top. This protocorm later develops into the roots and into the first leaves of the orchid, a process that sometimes takes several years. During this prolonged stage, the orchid is totally dependent on the mycorrhizal fungus for nutrition. This relationship lasts at least until the orchid develops its first leaves and becomes photosynthetic.

Some orchids in the *Cypripedium* genus are virtually free of mycorrhizal fungus as adult plants (Whitlow 1983). However, most terrestrial orchids rely on this mycorrhizal relationship for a continued supply of min-

## Who Benefits?

The orchid clearly benefits from its mycorrhizal relationship, but apparently the fungus receives nothing in return, leading some authors to describe the orchid as a parasite on the fungus. However, recent research shows that the relationship between the orchid and its mycorrhizal partner is mutual and reciprocal, with both benefiting from the exchange of nutrients (Ospina 1996).

erals such as nitrogen and phosphorus—and sometimes for a substantial amount of their carbohydrates. Saprophytic orchids are incapable of photosynthesis and throughout their lives remain totally dependent on their symbiotic fungi for carbohydrate nutrition.

## Dormancy

Orchids in Texas and temperate North America must endure extremes of winter cold, summer heat, and drought. Like many perennial garden plants—including amaryllises, lilies, irises, and others—orchids endure adverse climatic and environmental conditions by entering a dormant state in which the aboveground parts die back. During the growing season, food and water are stored in swollen underground stems such as tubers, corms, or rhizomes. During the following growing season, or whenever environmental conditions are favorable, stored food and water are utilized to produce new orchid plants and flowers. Many terrestrial orchids such as *Calopogons* bear underground tubers or corms which are usually replaced annually. Some orchids, including the southern Lady's slipper *(Cypripedium kentuckiense),* the chatterbox orchid *(Epipactis gigantea),* the rose pogonia *(Pogonia ophioglossoides),* and several others, store water and nutrients in creeping rhizomes. In some cases, orchids can remain underground in a dormant state for several years and emerge aboveground when conditions are again favorable for growth. The orchid's mycorrhizal fungus may provide nutrients while the subterranean orchid is dormant.

## Soil: *The Firm Foundation*

The type of soil, its texture, structure, organic matter content, and pH, strongly influence the occurrence and distribution of many kinds of plants, especially orchids. These factors also greatly affect the availability of moisture and plant nutrients in the soil. Soil texture refers to the relative amounts of sand, silt, and clay that make up a soil. Soil structure is the physical arrangement of the soil particles. Together, these two properties determine the porosity of the soil and its ability to retain moisture. Soil pH, the degree of acidity or alkalinity, is perhaps the most important factor affecting where orchids grow. Calcareous soils derived from limestone, which contains calcium carbonate, are alkaline. Texas orchids that prefer calcareous soil include the chatterbox orchid *(Epipactis gigantea)*, the shadow witch *(Ponthieva racemosa)*, the Great Plains ladies tresses *(Spiranthes magnicamporum)*, and the crested coral root *(Hexalectris spicata* var. *spicata)*. Sandy soils are composed largely of quartz and tend to be acidic, especially in forested regions that receive plentiful rainfall. Pine needles, sphagnum moss, and peat (partially decomposed plant material) greatly increase soil acidity. Many bog orchids, including the rose pogonia *(Pogonia ophioglossoides)*, the grass pink *(Calopogon tuberosus)*, the yellow fringed orchid *(Platanthera ciliaris)*, the crested fringed orchid *(P. cristata)*, and the little club-spur orchid *(P. clavellata)*, thrive in highly acidic soil.

Besides being particular about soil type, many orchids are also particular about soil temperature. Having a particular soil temperature is critical for several native Texas orchids that also grow in the northern United States and Canada. In bogs, a constant supply of seepage water keeps the soil cool, protecting orchids from the heat of summer. Some orchids find the cool soil they need in the deep shade of the forest.

## SUN AND SHADE, SAVANNAH AND GLADE

Many orchids have specific light requirements. Orchids of the open bogs and meadows perish if they become

### "One Uniform Green Carpet Throughout the Globe"

Charles Darwin, in *Various Contrivances by Which Orchids Are Fertilised by Insects*, was the first writer to document the incredible numbers of seeds produced by a single orchid flower. Darwin estimated that a single seed pod of the European *Orchis maculata* produced more than 30 seedpods containing 6,200 seeds each, for a total of approximately 186,000 seeds. However, this is a modest number compared to the capsule of the tropical orchid *Maxillaria*, with its 2 million seeds.

Darwin wrote: "To give an idea of what the above figures mean, I will briefly show the possible rate of increase of *Orchis maculata*: an acre of land would hold 174,240 plants, each having a space of six inches square, and this would be just sufficient for their growth: so that making the fair allowance of 400 bad seeds in each capsule, an acre would be thickly clothed by the progeny of a single plant. At the same rate of increase, the grandchildren would cover a space slightly exceeding the island of Anglesea; and the great grandchildren of a single plant would nearly (in the ratio of 47 to 50) clothe with one uniform green carpet the entire surface of the land throughout the globe."

shaded by trees and shrubs. On the other hand, woodland orchids often die from too much light when the
forest canopy is removed by clear cutting, selective cutting, or storms.

## USURPED SPECIES AND THE
## SUCCESSION OF SURVIVORS

Although it is not often apparent to the human observer,
the vegetation of any landscape is continually chang-
ing. This includes orchid habitats. Many orchid species can be abundant at a particular site for several years,
but conspicuously absent in subsequent years. Orchids
can also appear suddenly in locations where they were
unknown before.

Such changes can often be attributed to vegetational
changes associated with a process called *plant succession*. Plant succession is set in motion by natural events
such as storms, fires, floods, and erosion, or by human
activities such as timber cutting, bulldozing, and exca-
vating soil. These catastrophic events destroy much of
the plant cover in an area, exposing patches of unvege-
tated soil. In the early stages of plant succession, "pioneer plants" sprout from seed and become established
as a new plant community on this newly exposed soil.
As the process continues, this community and each
succeeding plant community replaces another as environmental conditions change. For example, as one particular plant community matures, its growth may contribute to changes in light level, organic content of the
soil, and the ability of the site to retain moisture. Eventually, a "late-successional" community is reached and
becomes self-perpetuating. These stable communities
can persist indefinitely, or at least until the next catastrophic event. Many native orchids are not late-
successional species, but are plants of transient stages
of succession that invade favorable sites, flourish for a
while, and then disappear when the habitat changes
(Case 1987). However, the southern Lady's slipper *(Cypripedium kentuckiense)* and a few other species can be
regarded as late-successional species.

## THE ROLE OF DISTURBANCE
## IN ORCHID HABITATS

Fred Case, author of *Orchids of the Western Great Lakes Region* (1987), was the first botanist to recognize the role of disturbance in maintaining ideal habitats for some orchid species. Intolerant of competition from other plants, some orchid species favor habitats that are subjected to recurrent disturbances, such as periodic fires, flooding, grazing and trampling by animals, and erosion, all of which continually remove much of the competing vegetation and expose fresh soil.

Orchids that are adapted to disturbed sites include the shadow witch *(Ponthieva racemosa),* the rose pogonia *(Pogonia ophioglossoides),* members of the genus *Calopogon,* and several other species. The shadow witch, for example, favors deep ravines that are subject to continuous erosion and water seepage, a situation that is stressful to many other plants. The rose pogonia typically thrives in sites that are continuously saturated by percolating ground water. It, along with members of the *Calopogon* genus, also prefers areas that experience periodic fires.

# THE NATURAL REGIONS OF TEXAS

The interplay between various soil types, climates, and landforms has resulted in several distinct natural vegetation regions in Texas. Various authors (Gould et al. 1960, Correll and Johnston 1979, Hatch et al. 1990) have divided Texas into ten different natural regions, each characterized by its own particular mixture of vegetation. These regions are:

- Pineywoods
- Gulf Prairies and Marshes
- Post Oak Savannah
- Blackland Prairies
- Cross Timbers and Prairies
- South Texas Plains
- Edwards Plateau
- Rolling Plains
- High Plains
- Trans-Pecos Texas

The vegetation of each region is usually homogeneous; however, local environmental conditions can sometimes result in vegetation that is uncharacteristic of the region. Much of the original vegetation of these specific regions has been altered by human activities, and distinctions are not as clearly defined as they once were. Despite these changes, the various vegetation regions provide a logical format for a discussion of the distribution of orchids in Texas. Each orchid species description in this book includes the specific vegetation regions where that orchid occurs.

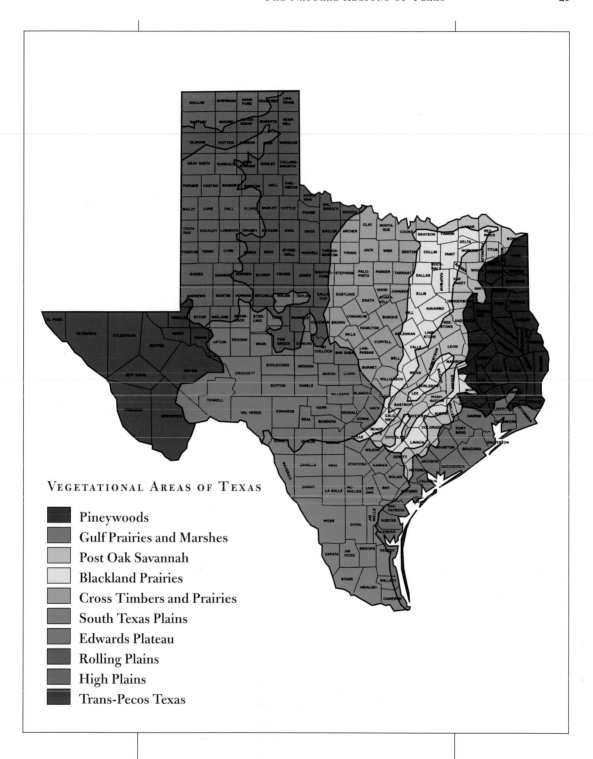

VEGETATIONAL AREAS OF TEXAS

- Pineywoods
- Gulf Prairies and Marshes
- Post Oak Savannah
- Blackland Prairies
- Cross Timbers and Prairies
- South Texas Plains
- Edwards Plateau
- Rolling Plains
- High Plains
- Trans-Pecos Texas

FIGURE 2
Vegetational areas
of Texas

## PINEYWOODS

The Pineywoods region, located in the extreme eastern part of the state, extends west from the Louisiana border about 75 to 125 miles into Texas. This botanically diverse region is dissected by many streams, and the terrain varies from gently rolling to hilly. Sandy soil and sandy loam, together with abundant rainfall, support extensive pine-hardwood forests, longleaf-pine uplands, wetland pine savannahs, hillside seepage bogs, baygalls, and swamps.

## GULF PRAIRIES AND MARSHES

The Gulf Prairies and Marshes region consists of a narrow strip of nearly level land 30 to 80 miles wide that skirts the coast of the Gulf of Mexico from the Sabine River to the Rio Grande. Before extensive industrial, agricultural, and residential development, this region consisted mostly of vast tallgrass prairies and post oak savannah. Salt, brackish, and fresh marshes of this region form a thin band along the coast. In some areas, alluvial bottomlands are timbered in rich hardwood forests of live oak, water oak, and other oaks and hardwoods. Soils in this region are primarily clays and clayey loams.

## POST OAK SAVANNAH

The Post Oak Savannah region, a mixture of hardwood forests and tallgrass prairies, lies to the west of and is adjacent to the Pineywoods region. This gently rolling to hilly plain is forested with post oak, blackjack oak, hickory, elm, hackberry, and juniper. Soils of this region are shallow, sandy loams that are underlain by a clayey subsoil.

## BLACKLAND PRAIRIES

The Blackland Prairies region lies to the west of the Post Oak Savannah region, although two small strips of Blackland Prairies are interspersed with the southern

Post Oak Savannah region. Humus-rich, dark clay soils once supported vast tallgrass prairies of little bluestem grass, big bluestem, Indiangrass, switchgrass, tall dropseed, and silver dropseed. Such soil is ideally suited for farming, and consequently, little remains of these prairies today. Numerous streams in the Blackland Prairies region are wooded with a variety of oaks, pecan, cedar elm, hackberry, bois d'arc, and mesquite.

## Cross Timbers and Prairies

The Cross Timbers and Prairies region is located in north Central Texas, west of the Blackland Prairies region. This region, ranging from rolling to hilly country, consists of alternate bands of tallgrass prairies and stunted woodlands of post oak, blackjack oak, live oak, and juniper. Soils vary from prairie soils made up of calcareous clays to sandy loams in the wooded Cross Timbers.

## South Texas Plains

The South Texas Plains range from the Rio Grande in the south up to the southern edge of the Edwards Plateau, and then eastward to the Gulf Prairies and Marshes region along the Gulf Coast. This region, which varies from level land to gently rolling hills, contains prairie grasslands and brushy woodlands of mesquite, live oak, acacia, Brazil, spiny hackberry, whitebrush, lime prickly ash, Texas persimmon, and other small trees and shrubs. Heavy cattle grazing and suppression of naturally occurring fires have resulted in a great increase in woody brush species.

## Edwards Plateau

The Edwards Plateau region, also known as the "Texas Hill Country," is located in central and southwest Texas. The Balcones Escarpment, which is cut by a series of rugged canyons, marks the southern and eastern boundaries of this region. The northern and western boundaries of the Edwards Plateau are less apparent where they grade into other regions. Shallow soils overlying limestone support tallgrass, mid-grass, and shortgrass prairies with scattered woodlands of plateau live oak, shin oak, mesquite, and juniper.

## ROLLING PLAINS

The Texas Panhandle comprises the Rolling Plains region and the High Plains region. The Rolling Plains region is abruptly separated from the High Plains by the steep cliffs of the Caprock Escarpment. The Rolling Plains display a gently rolling to moderately hilly topography. Coarse sand, red clays, and shales form several different soil types in this region. Tallgrass and mixed-grass prairies of little bluestem, big bluestem, sideoats grama, Indiangrass, switchgrass, hairy grama, blue grama, Canada rye, and western wheatgrass once stretched across this region. Well suited for grazing, much of this region is now devoted to cattle ranching; little remains of the original prairies.

## HIGH PLAINS

The High Plains region, a nearly level, high, treeless plain, occupies the western portion of the Texas Panhandle. The vegetation of the High Plains originally consisted mostly of mixed-grass and shortgrass prairies. Soils of this region range from clays to sands that are usually underlain by calcium carbonate–cemented sands and gravels. Today, much of this region is cultivated farmland and cattle ranches.

## TRANS-PECOS TEXAS

The Trans-Pecos region, made up of mountains, arid valleys, and dry desert, occupies the far western part of Texas west of the Pecos River. The vegetation of this region is diverse, varying from low desert to wooded mountain slopes and coniferous and hardwood forests at high elevations.

# How TEXAS ORCHID HABITATS ARE DESCRIBED IN THIS BOOK

Those who want to find wild orchids must learn to recognize the habitats where orchids grow and to identify the kinds of plants that thrive alongside them. Texas orchid habitat descriptions in this book are based on herbarium records, personal observations in the field, and reports from botanical literature. Individual orchid habitats are classified as forests, woodlands, savannahs, prairies, swamps, marshes, bogs, and seeps. Each is characterized by the types of plant species found there.

- A forest is a community of trees with crowns forming an almost continuous canopy.

- A woodland is a community of widely spaced trees that form a broken canopy.

- A savannah is a grass-dominated community with widely scattered trees and shrubs.

- A prairie is a grassland in which trees are largely absent.

- A swamp is a forest, woodland, or shrubland with standing water for much of the year.

- A marsh is a grass and herb-dominated community with standing water for most of the year.

- A bog is an area of spongy, waterlogged ground characterized by acid-loving plants such as sphagnum moss, sedges, grasses, and flowering herbs.

- A seep is an area where there is a slow, steady flow of groundwater from porous soil or rock, usually a hillside or stream bank. Seeps support a variety of woodland plants, including sedges, grasses, ferns, and wildflowers. The types of vegetation that grow on seeps can vary greatly, depending upon whether they are found on alkaline soils or acidic soils.

Plant communities do not always fall into neat categories, but often overlap. This sometimes makes it difficult to assign orchids to specific habitats. While many orchid species are restricted to distinct habitats, some can grow in a variety of habitats. Also, some orchids thrive in transition zones between habitats.

Native plant habitats of Texas are classified into an assortment of names by different authors. The most complete classification system for plant communities in Texas is "A Framework for Plant Community Classification and Conservation in Texas" (Diamond et al. 1987). In our habitat descriptions, we include plant community names from this system along with names used by other botanists, and provide citations for each.

# ORCHIDS OF THE
# BOGS AND SAVANNAHS

A rainbow of seldom-seen orchids grow in the soggy wetlands of East Texas, sometimes not too far from the popular woodland trails. These wetlands can be home to great displays of Texas orchids and have the added enticement of insectivorous plants and colorful wildflowers, grasses, and sedges. Once extensive in the Big Thicket region, most boggy wetlands have been drained out, cleared off, and filled in to be replaced by pastures, housing developments, and pine plantations.

Of the many types of wetlands in East Texas, three are particularly important for orchids: wetland pine savannahs, hillside seepage bogs, and baygalls. These three distinct plant communities, often collectively called bogs, have many features in common. Their soil is often waterlogged, but is seldom covered with deep standing water. High rainfall and continuous seepage leach many nutrients from the porous soil, leaving it sterile and acidic. The water percolating through these wetlands is low in oxygen, which hinders the breakdown of organic matter and the release of important plant nutrients. Sphagnum moss often grows here.

## WETLAND PINE SAVANNAHS

The first type of wetland, the wetland pine savannah, is found primarily in the Pineywoods vegetation region on the flatter areas of the Gulf coastal plain in southeast Texas. A wetland pine savannah is a flat grassland with widely scattered longleaf pines *(Pinus palustris)* and small trees and shrubs, including black gum *(Nyssa sylvatica* var. *biflora),* sweetbay magnolia *(Magnolia virginiana),* wax myrtle *(Myrica* spp.), and black titi *(Cyrilla racemiflora).* The open canopy of longleaf pines admits enough sunlight to support herbaceous species such as beakrush *(Rhynchospora* spp.), sedge *(Carex* spp.), and grasses such as little bluestem *(Schizachyrium scoparium), Panicum* spp., and *Paspalum* spp. This type of habitat supports a diversity of orchids, including the snowy orchid *(Platanthera nivea),* the Chapman's orchid *(P. chapmanii),* the grass pink *(Calopogon tuberosus),* the rose pogonia *(Pogonia ophioglossoides),* the giant ladies tresses *(Spiranthes praecox),* the nodding ladies tresses *(S. cernua),* and the spring ladies tresses *(S. vernalis).* Rare orchids such as the Oklahoma grass pink *(Calopogon oklahomensis),* the giant spiral orchid *(Spiranthes longilabris),* and the Florida ladies tresses *(S. brevilabris* var. *floridana)* are found sparingly in this habitat. Colorful wildflowers found here include meadow beauty *(Rhexia mariana* and *R. lutea),* gay feather *(Liatris* spp.), milkwort *(Polygala* spp.), yellow-eyed grasses *(Xyris* spp.), pine-woods rose-gentian

Wetland pine savannah habitat of ***Platanthera nivea*** snowy orchid

*(Sabatia gentianoides),* and colic root *(Aletris aurea).* Carnivorous plants flourish in the sterile and often saturated soil in these grassy longleaf pinelands. Pitcher plants *(Sarracenia alata)* may grow in the wetland pine savannahs on the Bentley geological formation, but are not found in most southeast Texas wetland pine savannahs.

Underlying the wetland pine savannahs are impermeable layers of cemented sand and clay that impede drainage and cause a high water table in winter and spring, and during periods of heavy rainfall.

These boggy open pinelands were once extensive on broad flat terraces of the outer coastal plain in much of Hardin, Jasper, Newton, and Tyler Counties (Watson 1979, Bridges and Orzell 1989b). Now, fewer than ten good examples of this habitat remain in East Texas and western Louisiana. The only protected wetland pine savannahs are on public lands in the Big Thicket National Preserve. A program of prescribed burns is vital to the survival of the ones that remain. Wetland pine savannahs (Marks and Harcombe 1981) are also known by several other names, including pine savannah wetlands (Watson 1979), longleaf–black gum savannahs (Ajilvsgi 1979), wetland longleaf pine savannahs (Bridges and Orzell 1989b), and longleaf pine–beakrush series communities (Diamond et al. 1987).

## Orchids of the Wetland Pine Savannahs

*Calopogon oklahomensis*    Oklahoma grass pink
*C. tuberosus*    grass pink
*Platanthera chapmanii*    Chapman's orchid
*P. cristata*    crested fringed orchid
*P. integra*    golden frog arrow
*P. nivea*    snowy orchid
*Pogonia ophioglossoides*    rose pogonia
*Spiranthes brevilabris* var. *brevilabris*
    Texas ladies tresses
*S. brevilabris* var. *floridana*    Florida ladies tresses
*S. cernua*    nodding ladies tresses
*S. longilabris*    giant spiral orchid
*S. praecox*    giant ladies tresses
*S. vernalis*    spring ladies tresses

## HILLSIDE SEEPAGE BOGS

The second type of wetland is the hillside seepage bog, also called a hanging bog. Plant life in hillside seepage bogs is almost identical to that found in wetland pine savannahs, and some authors classify them as the same habitat type (Watson 1979). Kept wet by a continuous supply of seeping water from springs and drained by

small streams farther downhill, hillside seepage bogs contain a top layer of wet sand and an underlying layer of impermeable clay or rock. In a lush growth of sphagnum moss, scattered clumps of insect-eating pitcher plants *(Sarracenia alata)* stand out like reptilian totems. They are often surrounded by other carnivorous plants such as sundew (*Drosera* spp.), butterwort *(Pinguicula pumila),* and bladderwort (*Utricularia* spp.). The rose pogonia *(Pogonia ophioglossoides)* and the grass pink *(Calopogon tuberosus),* the most frequently encountered orchids, often bloom in profusion. These two orchids grow in most hillside seepage bogs in the Pineywoods and in many of these types of bogs in the Post Oak Savannah region. They thrive in the open, sunny areas along with milkwort (*Polygala* spp.), gay feather *(Liatris pynostachya),* yellow-eyed grasses (*Xyris* spp.), pipewort *(Lachnocaulon anceps)* and (*Eriocaulon* spp.), grasses, sedges (*Carex* spp.), and beakrush (*Rhynchospora* spp.). The golden frog arrow *(Platanthera integra),* extremely rare in Texas, is known from just two such hillside seepage bogs.

Farther down the hill, royal fern *(Osmunda regalis),* cinnamon fern *(O. cinnamomea),* and broadleaf and evergreen shrubs—also found in baygalls—may prevail. The yellow fringed orchid *(Platanthera ciliaris)* is usually found here; so is the crested fringed orchid *(P. cristata),* but it is much more rare.

Hillside seepage bogs, found farther inland from the coast than the wetland pine savannahs, occur in more rolling terrain in the Pineywoods of East and southeast Texas and in the Post Oak Savannah region of central East Texas. In upland longleaf-pine or pine-oak forests, clusters of small hillside seepage bogs, each less than 5 acres, may be found.

Newton and Jasper Counties have the greatest number of hillside seepage bogs in Texas. The richest examples are at the Willis/Catahoula Formation contact in the south part of Angelina National Forest, where sand of the Willis Formation overlies an impermeable clay layer of the Catahoula Formation. Botanists Steve Orzell and Edwin Bridges found at least ninety-nine hillside seepage bogs in East Texas and western Louisiana in a survey during the 1980s, but they noted that two thirds of those wetlands were threatened by activities such as cattle grazing, ditch digging, and extinguishing of natural fires (Bridges and Orzell 1989b). Many good examples of hillside seepage bogs are preserved in the Upland Island Wilderness Area of Angelina National Forest. Other good examples are found in several Research Natural Areas and in Botanical Areas of Angelina National Forest and Sabine National Forest. Hillside seepage bogs are also referred to as hillside seepage herb bogs, seepage slopes (Bridges and Orzell 1989b), pitcher plant bogs (Nixon and Ward 1986), and a sphagnum-beakrush series (Diamond et al. 1987).

## Orchids of the Hillside Seepage Bogs

*Calopogon oklahomensis*   Oklahoma grass pink
*C. tuberosus*   grass pink
*Habenaria repens*   water spider orchid
*Platanthera ciliaris*   yellow fringed orchid
*P. cristata*   crested fringed orchid
*P. integra*   golden frog arrow
*Pogonia ophioglossoides*   rose pogonia
*Spiranthes cernua*   nodding ladies tresses
*S. praecox*   giant ladies tresses
*S. vernalis*   spring ladies tresses

## Bᴀʏɢᴀʟʟs

The third type of wetland, the baygall, is a mixed deciduous and evergreen forest located at the head of a stream, in a wet creek bottom, or in an abandoned stream channel. In a baygall, a constant supply of seepage water and poor drainage result in permanently saturated soil and pools of standing water. Baygalls often grade into either a wetland pine savannah, a hillside seepage bog, or a moist pine-hardwood forest. Sun-loving orchids, intolerant of the deep shade cast by the dense canopy within baygalls, often inhabit the more open transition zones around the outer edges. Here, the yellow fringed orchid *(Platanthera ciliaris),* crested fringed orchid *(P. cristata),* rose pogonia *(Pogonia ophioglossoides),* and grass pink *(Calopogon tuberosus)* often grow among the thick mats of sphagnum moss. The rare whorled pogonia orchid *(Isotria verticillata)* and green adder's mouth orchid *(Malaxis unifolia)* usually grow where the upper edges of baygalls grade into drier pine-hardwood forests. Also found here is the

A baygall in the Upland Island Wilderness Area, Angelina National Forest

Outer edges of baygalls are the habitat of *Platanthera ciliaris* yellow fringed orchid.

southern twayblade *(Listera australis)*. More tolerant of deep shade and saturated soil, the little club-spur orchid *(Platanthera clavellata)* thrives along shaded streams and in standing water in baygalls.

Baygalls are named for the sweetbay magnolia *(Magnolia virginiana)* and gallberry holly *(Ilex coriacea)*, which are often the dominant woody species, along with swamp red bay *(Persea borbonia)*, black gum *(Nyssa sylvatica* var. *biflora)*, and sweetgum *(Liquidambar styraciflua)*. The dense evergreen shrubbery of baygalls is comprised of possumhaw viburnum *(Viburnum nudum)*, puncture vine *(Smilax laurifolia)*, Virginia sweetspire *(Itea virginica)*, and bayberry *(Myrica heterophylla)* (Bridges and Orzell 1989b). Baygalls occur mainly in the East Texas Pineywoods. The lowest layer of vegetation, the ground cover, is often abundant with sedges such as *Carex* spp., *Eleocharis tortilis*, and *Rhynchospora mixta;* and with ferns such as netted chain fern *(Woodwardia areolata)*, cinnamon fern *(Osmunda cinnamomea)*, royal fern *(O. regalis)*, and Virginia chain fern *(Woodwardia virginica)* (Bridges and Orzell 1989b). Baygalls are also

*Lance Rosier watched them go one by one, the orchid bogs and the stands of insectivorous plants, the heron rookeries and the thick, magnolia-studded woods, the wild places he had known as a boy where you could hear nothing but frogs, birds, and the thunder of wind in big trees.*

A. Y. GUNTER
(*The Big Thicket*, 1971)

It is remarkable
that this, one of the
fairest of all our
flowers, should also
be one of the rarest—
for the most part not
seen at all. . . . The
village belle never
sees this more
delicate belle of the
swamp. . . . A
beauty reared in the
shade of a convent,
who has never
strayed beyond the
convent bell. Only
the skunk or the owl,
or other inhabitant
of the swamp,
beholds it.

HENRY DAVID
THOREAU
(*Summer* 1884)

called wet creek bottoms (Nixon et al. 1983), baygalls and acid bogs (Watson 1979), bay-gallberry holly bogs (Ajilvsgi 1979), semi-ever-green broadleaf acid seep forests (Bridges and Orzell 1989b), and sweetbay magnolia series forests (Diamond et al. 1987). Baygalls are still numerous in East Texas, but only a few are protected. These are located in the Big Thicket National Preserve; in Angelina National Forest (Upland Island Wilderness Area); in Research Natural Areas and in Botanical Areas in Angelina, Sabine, and Sam Houston National Forests.

## Orchids of the Baygalls

| | |
|---|---|
| *Habenaria repens* | water spider orchid |
| *Isotria verticillata* | whorled pogonia |
| *Listera australis* | southern twayblade |
| *Malaxis unifolia* | green adder's mouth |
| *Platanthera ciliaris* | yellow fringed orchid |
| *P. clavellata* | little club-spur orchid |
| *P. cristata* | crested fringed orchid |
| *P. flava* var. *flava* | southern rein orchid |
| *P. lacera* | ragged-fringed orchid |

## FROM BLAZES TO BLOOMS

On a cool January morning in East Texas, the reddish orange blaze of a morning fire sweeps through a forest of longleaf pines, consuming an accumulation of dead grasses and pine needles and an encroaching under-brush of shrubs. A tragedy? A disaster? Not necessarily. Look at the same sandy forest floor eight months after the fire. It is hot again, but the source of the heat is sun, not fire. A bright blaze of color reappears, but this time in the blooms of a golden frog arrow *(Platanthera integra)* on a tall, leafy stalk.

Botanists Steve Orzell and Edwin Bridges discovered this orchid in a hillside seepage bog in Angelina National Forest near Jasper on August 26, 1988. Until Orzell and Bridges spotted the golden frog arrow, it had not been scientifically documented in Texas for many years.[*] They had been surveying this hillside for several years, but the orchid did not appear until after the fire.

Another rare orchid, the Oklahoma grass pink *(Calo-pogon oklahomensis),* was observed by botanist Geraldine Watson for the first time in the Big Thicket after two fires in Kirby State Forest and the Hickory Creek Savannah Unit of the Big Thicket National Preserve (pers. com. 1979). It was considered to be *C. barbatus,*

**\*NOTE:** The only authentic historical record of *P. integra* in Texas was a collection made in 1950 by Mrs. J. L. Hooks from Hardin County (Bridges and Orzell 1989a). *P. integra* has been included in the flora of Texas by Oakes Ames (1924) and Donovan Correll (1944). The Ames and Correll accounts were based on a collection from Texas by Thomas Drummond. However, according to W. C. Holmes (1983), the Drummond specimens were misidentified, and are actually *P. nivea.*

but was later described by Douglas Goldman (1995) as a new species.

For many years, naturalists have observed the prolific blooming of some species of terrestrial orchids after fires. Donovan Correll (1950) noted that *Calopogons,* particularly the many-flowered grass pink *(C. multiflorous),* not only survive fires, but thrive "with vigor and freshness" in the blackened earth of burned pine savannahs. Response to fire varies among different orchid species. Some bloom only after a fire, while others bloom more readily after fire and continue to bloom for at least a few years afterward. Another group of orchid species seems indifferent to the effects of fire and blooms with or without fire (Dressler 1981). Flowering after burning has been observed in many herbs and grasses with underground storage organs such as tubers, bulbs, corms, and rhizomes (Stewart et al. 1982). Whether fire affects inconspicuous nonflowering plants or dormant subterranean ones is not known (Sheviak 1974). However, orchids with large starch reserves stored in tubers, corms, and rhizomes, and perhaps with the aid of mycorrhizal fungi, can persist underground in a dormant state for many years. Orchids that benefit from periodic fires include rose pogonia *(Pogonia ophioglossoides),* grass pink *(Calopogon tuberosus),* yellow fringed orchid *(Platanthera ciliaris),* Chapman's orchid *(P. chapmanii),* snowy orchid *(P. nivea),* and several species of ladies tresses *(Spiranthes* spp.).

What we commonly view as a disaster, a forest fire, sometimes creates perfect conditions for the growth of rare native orchids. In fact, several wild orchids and rare herbs that inhabit wetland pine savannahs and hillside seepage bogs actually depend on frequent fires in longleaf pine forests for survival. Many orchids and sun-loving herbs cannot survive in the shade created by a shrubby underbrush of wax myrtle *(Myrica* sp.), sweetbay magnolia *(Magnolia virginiana),* gallberry holly *(Ilex coriacea),* and black gum *(Nyssa sylvatica* var. *biflora).* Fire controls these shade-creating plants by arresting the process of plant succession and letting in sunlight. The result is a luxuriant growth of orchids, ferns, mosses, and bog-loving plants, including carnivo-

rous plants such as pitcher plant *(Sarracenia alata)*, sundew *(Drosera* sp.), butterwort *(Pinguicula pumila)*, and bladderwort *(Utricularia* sp.). In addition, fire restores minerals liberated from the ashes of consumed plant debris, particularly potassium, calcium, magnesium, and phosphorous—the very nutrients the water-leached acid soil lacks.

It is not only the smaller plants, such as orchids and herbs, that thrive in savannahs maintained by fire; the seed-bearing cone of the longleaf pine must be charred if the seeds are to sprout later. Longleaf pines, with needles well above the reach of most fires, are usually unharmed by typical low-intensity ground fires. Frequently, the fires are ignited by lightning and spread quickly, so that the longleaf pines are not badly damaged. Longleaf needles on the forest floor provide a ready supply of combustible material that keeps the flames moving along rapidly while generating little heat, and the seeds and roots of orchids and herbs are insulated from the heat by the loose, sandy soil.

Frequent fires have always been part of the natural history of the longleaf pine forests of the South. In pre-settlement days, vast, unbroken longleaf pine forests stretched across East Texas. Frequent wildfires caused by lightning crept across miles of pineland. When pioneers settled the area, the land became fragmented by farms, roads, and towns, all but eliminating natural wildfire.

Without fire, a longleaf pine savannah gradually changes through plant succession and eventually becomes a closed-canopy pine and oak forest. Wildflowers typical of hillside seepage bogs and wetland pine savannahs are gradually eliminated. Prescribed burns are now used to maintain longleaf pine forests in the Big Thicket National Preserve, Angelina National Forest, and Sabine National Forest. Periodic fires are also vital for maintaining prairies and other grasslands, and serve as a useful management tool.

OPPOSITE PAGE
The golden frog arrow *(Plantanthera integra)* reappeared after a fire.

# ORCHIDS OF OPEN SUNNY HABITATS

## ORCHIDS OF THE PRAIRIES AND MEADOWS

*P*rairies are usually not particularly rich in orchid species. Orchids that inhabit prairies are primarily widespread species that occur in open sunny sites in eastern North America (Sheviak 1983). Ladies tresses, members of the *Spiranthes* genus, are the most prominent orchid species found in Texas prairies. Intolerant of competition from other herbaceous plants, several members of this genus are colonizers of disturbed, sparsely vegetated areas. These orchids often appear on newly disturbed sites such as graded roadsides and cleared fields. The orchids then increase in number and flourish until crowded out by competing vegetation. With continued disturbances that suspend succession, including mowing, grazing, and burning, ladies tresses may thrive at a site indefinitely (Sheviak 1982).

Although little remains of the original prairies that once covered vast stretches of Texas, ladies tresses still grow in prairie remnants, pastures, vacant lots, and roadsides, especially in the Gulf Prairies and Marshes, the Post Oak Savannah, and the Blackland Prairies regions. In fact, a few of these ladies tresses species may be more common today because of large-scale human disturbances. The spring ladies tresses *(S. vernalis)*

### Orchids of the Prairies and Meadows

*Platanthera nivea*    snowy orchid
*Spiranthes brevilabris* var. *brevilabris*
    Texas ladies tresses
*S. cernua*    nodding ladies tresses
*S. lacera* var. *gracilis*
    southern slender ladies tresses
*S. magnicamporum*    Great Plains ladies tresses
*S. praecox*    giant ladies tresses
*S. tuberosa*    little ladies tresses
*S. vernalis*    spring ladies tresses

is particularly common in spring, especially in prairies and open areas in the eastern half of the state. Also abundant, mostly in sandy soil, is the fall-blooming nodding ladies tresses *(S. cernua)*. The southern slender ladies tresses *(S. lacera* var. *gracilis)* is rather common in prairie remnants and abandoned farmland of the Post Oak Savannah region. It also occurs in both the Blackland Prairies and the Gulf Prairies and Marshes region, but it is not as common. Often growing near *S. vernalis,* the giant ladies tresses *(S. praecox)* is frequent in the Gulf Prairies and Marshes region. However, it is not found in the Blackland Prairies region.

## ORCHIDS OF THE PINEYWOOD MEADOWS

Several species of ladies tresses *(Spiranthes)* are found in open meadows, in prairie inclusions, and near human-made clearings in the moist forests of the Pineywoods region. The spring ladies tresses *(S. vernalis),* the giant ladies tresses *(S. praecox),* and the nodding ladies tresses *(S. cernua)* are especially common on roadsides and in clearings throughout the region. The southern slender ladies tresses *(S. lacera* var. *gracilis)* also occurs frequently, particularly in the western part of the Pineywoods region. Preferring open sunny sites, these orchids are very rare in the deep shade of the forest.

---

### Orchids of the Pineywood Meadows

*Spiranthes brevilabris* var. *brevilabris*
   Texas ladies tresses
*S. cernua*   nodding ladies tresses
*S. lacera* var. *gracilis*
   southern slender ladies tresses
*S. magnicamporum*   Great Plains ladies tresses
*S. praecox*   giant ladies tresses
*S. tuberosa*   little ladies tresses
*S. vernalis*   spring ladies tresses

# ORCHIDS OF FORESTS AND WOODLANDS

## ORCHIDS OF THE MOIST PINE-HARDWOOD FORESTS

The greatest number of forest-dwelling orchids grow in the moist pine-hardwood forests of the Pineywoods region of East Texas, where the average rainfall is over 50 inches a year. The richest forests lie in the gently rolling-to-hilly terrain near the Louisiana border, where hundreds of spring-fed creeks wind. Evergreen trees such as the loblolly pine *(Pinus taeda),* the shortleaf pine *(P. echinata),* and the southern magnolia *(Magnolia grandiflora)* grow here along with a variety of hardwoods, including oak (*Quercus* spp.) and hickory (*Carya* spp.). The area is heavily forested with several trees typical of the deciduous forests of the eastern United States: American beech *(Fagus grandiflora),* white oak *(Quercus alba),* sugar maple *(Acer saccharum),* dogwood *(Cornus florida),* red maple *(Acer rubrum),* fringe tree *(Chionanthus virginica),* silverbell *(Halesia carolina),* snowbell *(Styrax americana),* and witch hazel *(Hamamelis virginiana).* These lush forests provide rich, moist leaf mulch and cool shade, and are home to the southern twayblade *(Listera australis),* the spring coral root *(Corallorhiza wisteriana),* and the cranefly orchid *(Tipularia discolor),* which are widespread and common throughout the region. The southern Lady's slipper *(Cypripedium kentuckiense),* whorled pogonia *(Isotria verticillata),* green adder's mouth *(Malaxis unifolia),* crested coral root *(Hexalectris spicata* var. *spicata),* and three birds orchid *(Triphora trianthophora)* are much more rare in these forests. These forest-dwelling orchids often grow in the company of trillium *(Trillium gracile),* bloodroot *(Sanguinaria canadensis),* jack-in-the-pulpit *(Arisaema* spp.), mayapple *(Podophyllum peltatum),* and trout lily *(Erythronium rostratum),* all plants that are characteristic of the eastern and Appalachian forests (Watson 1979). Many of these forest wildflowers and orchids reach their western limits in the forests of the Pineywoods region.

Unfortunately, none of the forest orchids are as common today as they once were. The rich forest they prefer once covered several million acres of East Texas, but only a few thousand acres of relatively undisturbed old-growth forest remain. A diversity of pine-hardwood forest types exists in the Pineywoods region of East Texas. These forests are classified as slope forests (Marks and Harcombe 1981), beech-magnolia-loblolly pine forests (Watson 1979), beech-magnolia-loblolly slopes (Ajilvsgi 1979), mesic uplands (Nixon 1985), American beech–southern magnolia series, American beech–white oak series, and loblolly pine–oak series forests (Diamond et al. 1987). A few good examples of this type of forest can still be seen in the Big Thicket National Preserve. Other good examples are in the Turkey Hill Wilderness Area

**Slope forest with Lady's slippers**

of Angelina National Forest, Indian Mounds Wilderness Area of Sabine National Forest, Big Creek Scenic Area in Sam Houston National Forest, and a few other natural and botanical research areas in the national forests that are protected by the U.S. Forest Service.

Southern Lady's slipper orchids *(Cypripedium kentuckiense)* are now extremely rare in Texas. Although this orchid was never abundant, it was once more common in the rich forests of East Texas. The late Osa Hall, a well-known forester and naturalist who lived in Newton County, remembered seeing it in profusion along spring-fed creeks in the beech forests when he was a boy in East Texas. In mid-April, the wooded slopes along streams glowed with the soft yellow of the southern Lady's slipper. As Hall grew older, he saw much of the beech forest disappear because of lumbering operations. In the 1960s, he found a few remaining stands of orchids, and even managed to rescue some of them in a huge washtub before a bulldozer destroyed their habitat. He gave them a new home on the moist banks of the stream that ran through his property, and every year he invited those who appreciated them to come and see his pride and joy in bloom.

## ORCHIDS OF THE FLOODPLAIN FORESTS

Floodplain forests are mostly confined to alluvial soil in the valleys of rivers and streams. These forests are periodically flooded from adjacent streams. Topographic features of floodplains include natural levees near the primary stream channels, forested bottomlands, terraces, ridges, and a network of sloughs, oxbow lakes, and swamps (Ajilvsgi 1979). Small differences in topography significantly affect the degree and regularity of flooding and the forest composition. Dominant trees in the floodplain forests of the Pineywoods region include sweetgum *(Liquidambar styraciflua)* and an

---

### Orchids of the Moist Pine-Hardwood Forests

*Corallorhiza wisteriana*     spring coral root

*Cypripedium kentuckiense*     southern Lady's slipper

*Hexalectris spicata* var. *spicata*     crested coral root

*Isotria verticillata*     whorled pogonia

*Listera australis*     southern twayblade

*Malaxis unifolia*     green adder's mouth

*Spiranthes ovalis*     oval ladies tresses

*Tipularia discolor*     cranefly orchid

*Triphora trianthophora*     three birds orchid

assortment of oaks such as water oak *(Quercus nigra),* willow oak *(Q. phellos),* swamp chestnut oak *(Q. michauxii),* cherrybark oak *(Q. falcata* var. *pagodifolia),* and overcup oak *(Q. lyrata)* (Ajilvsgi 1979, Marks and Harcombe 1981). Other important trees found in these forests are American hornbeam *(Carpinus caroliniana),* black gum *(Nyssa sylvatica),* and red maple *(Acer rubrum).*

Upper terraces of floodplain forests along smaller streams in the Pineywoods region represent transition areas where floodplain forests grade into moist pine-hardwood forests. These moist terraces often contain elements of adjacent pine-hardwood forests such as American holly *(Ilex ipaca),* loblolly pine *(Pinus taeda),* southern magnolia *(Magnolia grandiflora),* white oak *(Quercus alba),* and American beech *(Fagus grandiflora)* (Ajilvsgi 1979, Marks and Harcombe 1981). Upper floodplain terraces provide an ideal environment for the southern twayblade *(Listera australis),* the spring coral root *(Corallorhiza wisteriana),* the cranefly orchid *(Tipularia discolor),* and the elusive and rare three birds orchid *(Triphora trianthophora).*

The southern rein orchid *(Platanthera flava* var. *flava)* and the oval ladies tresses *(Spiranthes ovalis),* both very rare, often grow on lower, more frequently flooded terraces of floodplain forests. Baldcypress-tupelo swamps and sloughs, occurring in the lowest portions of the floodplains, are usually flooded for much of the year. Baldcypress *(Taxodium distichum),* with its large buttressed trunks and conspicuous knees, and water tupelo *(Nyssa aquatica),* with massive swollen bases, dominate these swamps. Large ash trees *(Fraxinus* spp.) are also an important component. The understory of these swamp forests is composed of a mixture of red maple *(Acer rubrum),* water elm *(Planera aquatica),* and buttonbush *(Cephalanthus occidentalis)* (Watson 1979). The fragrant ladies tresses *(Spiranthes odorata)* frequently

## Orchids of the Floodplain Forests

*Corallorhiza wisteriana*   spring coral root
*Listera australis*   southern twayblade
*Platanthera flava* var. *flava*
   southern rein orchid (lower terraces)
*Spiranthes odorata*
   fragrant ladies tresses (baldcypress-
   tupelo swamps and lower terraces)
*S. ovalis*   oval ladies tresses (lower terraces)
*Tipularia discolor*   cranefly orchid
*Triphora trianthophora*   three birds orchid

grows on patches of bare to scarcely vegetated mud and in shallow standing water on the banks of these sloughs and swamps. In this setting, the fragrant ladies tresses, with its exceptionally large spiraling blooms and large leafy plants, often forms large colonies around the bases and knees of cypresses. Other herbaceous plants found nearby include savannah panicum *(Panicum gymno-carpon)*, lizard's tail *(Saururus cernuus)*, and sensitive fern *(Onoclea sensibilis)*.

Floodplain forests of the Pineywoods are classified as sweetgum-oak floodplain forests (Ajilvsgi 1979), stream floodplain forests (Watson 1979), floodplain hardwood forests (Marks and Harcombe 1981), and water oak-sweetgum series (Diamond et al. 1987). Baldcypress-tupelo swamps are synonymous with swamp cypress tupelo forests (Marks and Harcombe 1981), cypress-tupelo swamps (Watson 1979), and bald-cypress series (Diamond et al. 1987).

## ORCHIDS OF DRY UPLAND FORESTS OF THE PINEYWOODS

Dry upland forests in the Pineywoods region occur on sandy, well-drained, gently rolling uplands between streams. Soils in these uplands often become excessively dry in summer and fall. There can be considerable regional variation in tree composition of these uplands. Post oak *(Quercus stellata)*, black hickory *(Carya texana)*, blackjack oak *(Q. marilandica)*, bluejack oak *(Q. incana)*, and black oak *(Q. velutina)* are usually the dominant trees in drier uplands, although pines are sometimes co-dominants (Nixon 1985). In southeast Texas, longleaf pine *(Pinus palustris)*, shortleaf pine *(P. echinata)*, or a combination of both, is often dominant in dry upland forests (Marks and Harcombe 1975, Bridges and Orzell 1989b). Shortleaf pine is the most prominent pine in the uplands of northeast Texas; longleaf pine does not occur there. Periodic fires are undoubtedly important factors in determining the tree composition in these dry uplands. Loblolly pine *(Pinus taeda)*, sweetgum *(Liquidambar styraciflua)*, and dogwood *(Cornus florida)* are often abundant in cutover

**Orchids of Dry Upland Forests
of the Pineywoods**

*Spiranthes cernua*    nodding ladies tresses
*S. lacera* var. *gracilis*
    southern slender ladies tresses
*S. parksii*
    Navasota ladies tresses (Jasper County)
*S. tuberosa*    little ladies tresses

and unburned upland woods in the Pineywoods region (Bridges and Orzell 1989b). Other trees in dry uplands may include red mulberry *(Morus rubra)*, southern red oak *(Quercus falcata)*, sassafras *(Sassafras albidum)*, woolly bumelia *(Bumelia lanuginosa)*, and winged elm *(Ulmus alata)*. Common understory shrubs in these uplands include yaupon *(Ilex vomitoria)*, farkleberry *(Vaccinium arboreum)*, American beautyberry *(Callicarpa americana)*, winged sumac *(Rhus copallina)*, and St. Andrews cross *(Ascyum hypericoides)* (Nixon 1985). The herbaceous ground layer in these uplands varies from a dense cover of grasses in moist sites to a sparsely vegetated sand in drier sites.

Dry uplands in the Pineywoods region are generally poor habitats for moisture-loving orchids. However, a few species of *Spiranthes* are tolerant of rather dry environments. The little ladies tresses *(S. tuberosa)*, well adapted to dry sandy soil, thrives in these rather dry upland forests and woodlands in the Pineywoods region. This tiny orchid, the smallest of the North American ladies tresses, blooms in June and July when the soil is dry. The southern slender ladies tresses *(S. lacera* var. *gracilis)* is also frequently found in upland forests in this region. Although more common in moist sites, the nodding ladies tresses *(S. cernua)* occasionally grows in dry uplands in the Pineywoods.

## ORCHIDS OF THE POST OAK SAVANNAH

Post oak *(Quercus stellata)* is by far the most prominent tree in the woodlands of the Post Oak Savannah region. Other major components of these woodlands are black hickory *(Carya texana)* and blackjack oak *(Q. marilandica)*. Understory species in the woodlands include yaupon *(Ilex vomitoria)*, winged elm *(Ulmus alata)*, farkleberry *(Vaccinium arboreum)*, sassafras *(Sassafras albidum)*, dogwood *(Cornus florida)*, summer grape *(Vitis aestivalis)*, and American beautyberry *(Callicarpa americana)* (Ward and Nixon 1992). The open woodlands of this region are interspersed with open prairies with tall grasses.

Woodlands of the Post Oak Savannah region have highly distinctive orchid flora. The rare Navasota ladies tresses *(Spiranthes parksii)* is a unique orchid in the region. This orchid is endemic to the Post Oak Savannah region, and, except for one disjunct (isolated) station in Jasper County in the Pineywoods region, occurs nowhere else in the world. This geographically restricted ladies tresses is on the U.S. List of Endangered and Threatened Species. It usually grows in open wooded margins along gravelly, slightly eroded creeks in woodlands composed of post oak and blackjack oak. It is often associated with yaupon, American beautyberry, and little bluestem grass *(Schizachyrum scoparium)* (Poole and Riskind 1987).

> **Orchids of the Post Oak Savannah**
>
> *Corallorhiza wisteriana*    spring coral root
> *Hexalectris spicata* var. *spicata*    crested coral root
> *Spiranthes cernua*    nodding ladies tresses
> *S. lacera* var. *gracilis*
>      southern slender ladies tresses
> *S. ovalis*    oval ladies tresses
> *S. parksii*    Navasota ladies tresses
> *S. tuberosa*    little ladies tresses
> *S. vernalis*    spring ladies tresses

Another ladies tresses orchid *(Spiranthes lacera* var. *gracilis)* is particularly abundant in the Post Oak Savannah woodlands of this region. This pioneer species is intolerant of tallgrasses and other competing plants, and thrives on disturbed, less densely vegetated sites. It often grows on mowed roadsides, in clearings on the edges of woods, and on abandoned farmland and pastures. The nodding ladies tresses *(S. cernua)* (both the typical open-flowered form and the closed-flowered form) is also plentiful in sandy, moist areas in the open woodlands of this region. The little ladies tresses *(S. tuberosa)* is also rather common in sandy openings on the edges of post oak woodlands. Although not particularly common, the spring ladies tresses *(S. vernalis)* is also found here. Two saprophytic orchids, the spring coral root *(Corallorhiza wisteriana)* and the crested coral root *(Hexalectris spicata* var. *spicata),* also grow in woodlands in the Post Oak Savannah region. Here they are occasionally found in deep leaf litter and in organic-rich sandy soil under yaupon, post oak, blackjack oak, and black hickory.

# ORCHIDS OF
# THE MOUNTAINS
# AND CANYONS

## TRANS-PECOS TEXAS
### *Where the Lone Star Sets*

Trans-Pecos Texas, a harsh and arid land, lies west of the Pecos River in the northern Chihuahuan Desert in far West Texas. Hardly anyone would expect to find water-loving orchids here, where the scorched, hot lowlands receive less than 8 inches of rain a year. But in the mountains, the temperature is considerably cooler and rainfall is more plentiful, with more than 20 inches a year at the highest elevations.

In Trans-Pecos Texas, orchids do thrive in the cool mountains, forested canyons, and riparian woodlands, places where they find precious moisture and refuge from the intense desert heat. In this region, the Chisos, Davis, Guadalupe, Glass, and Del Norte Mountains support oak-juniper-pinyon pine woodlands at middle elevations, mainly above 4,400 feet. Remnant conifer forests occur at the highest elevations in the Guadalupe, Davis, and Chisos Mountains. Each mountain range displays its own particular mixture of trees, resulting in considerable regional variation in the woodlands and forests (Powell 1988).

Oak-juniper-pinyon pine woodlands, composed of a mixture of oak (*Quercus* spp.), juniper (*Juniperus* spp.), Mexican pinyon pine *(Pinus cembroides)*, or Colorado pinyon *(P. edulis)*, are usually most developed on north-facing and east-facing slopes and in valleys. Cool, wet canyons in these woodlands commonly support Chisos red oak *(Quercus gravesii)*, Texas madrone *(Arbutus xalapensis)*, and bigtooth maple *(Acer grandi-*

dentatum) (Powell 1988). Montane conifer forests (pine-oak forests) that occur at higher elevations in the Guadalupe, Davis, and Chisos Mountains are considered by some biologists to be relicts of vast western coniferous forests of the Pleistocene. These forests are composed of ponderosa pine *(Pinus ponderosa)*, *P. arizonica,* Douglas fir *(Pseudotsuga menziesii),* southwestern white pine *(Pinus strobiformis),* quaking aspen *(Populus tremuloides),* and chinquapin oak *(Quercus muehlinbergii)* (Powell 1988). Many of the plants found here are characteristic of the forests of the Rocky Mountains (Warnock 1977).

Moist canyons in oak-juniper-pinyon pine woodlands are inhabited by five colorful orchids in the *Hexalectris* genus. These saprophytes grow in rich leaf mulch on the shaded forest floor. The curly coral root *(H. revoluta)* and the Glass Mountain coral root *(H. nitida)* are sometimes found together, although the curly coral root is more rare and usually blooms earlier. Found under Graves oak *(Quercus gravesii),* Texas madrone,

Several species thrive in the cool, moist woodlands of the Chisos Mountains, a mile above the forest floor.

and bigtooth maple in the Chisos Mountains, these orchids are usually restricted to more moist canyons. However, Barton Warnock (1977) found these orchids among lechuguilla *(Agave lechuguilla)* and shinnery oak *(Quercus havardii)* on sunny slopes in the Glass Mountains. The Texas purple spike (*H. warnockii*) is perhaps the most abundant *Hexalectris* orchid in the mountains of the Trans-Pecos. Although this orchid often resides in moist areas near streams and sometimes occurs with other *Hexalectris* orchids, it is surprisingly tolerant of dry, rocky soil and can grow in stunted oak groves and under pinyon pine. Botanist and nature writer Jean Hardy found it among shrub oaks in the arid Solitario in Presidio County (pers. com.). The giant coral root *(H. grandiflora)* is considered by many botanists, including Warnock, to be the most beautiful orchid in the Trans-Pecos. This brilliant rose pink sapro-

*Hexalectris warnockii*
Texas purple spike

phyte is largely confined to moist canyons, fern grot-
toes, waterfalls, and stream banks in the oak-juniper-
pinyon pine woodlands of the Davis Mountains in Jeff
Davis County. Although it thrives under Texas madrone and oak, it is also found under pinyon pine. The
crested coral root *(H. spicata* var. *spicata),* the most
wide-ranging member of the *Hexalectris* genus, appears
to be the rarest in the oak-juniper-pinyon pine woodlands of Trans-Pecos Texas. A few herbarium specimens
of this species from the Chisos Mountains and the
Guadalupe Mountains are the newly described self-
pollinating variety, *H. spicata* var. *arizonica* (Catling and
Engel 1993).

Four colorful ladies tresses orchids grow on open,
rocky stream banks in the Trans-Pecos. The striking
scarlet ladies tresses *(Dichromanthus cinnabarinus)*
thrives in several locations in the Chisos Mountains
and Glass Mountains. It frequently grows with sotol
*(Dasylirion* spp.), century plant *(Agave americana),* and
lechuguilla *(Agave* spp.) on grassy slopes along streams
and arroyos in oak-juniper-pinyon pine woodlands.
The fragrant, green-striped, Michoacan ladies tresses
*(Stenorrhynchos michuacanus)* is found in similar locations in the Chisos Mountains. Although there are no
recent records, this orchid was collected in the Chinati
Mountains of Presidio County by botanist Valery
Havard in 1880 (Correll 1944). The Hidalgo ladies
tresses *(Deiregyne confusa),* formerly known as *Spiranthes durangensis* (Garay 1980), was collected only
once in 1931 from the Chisos Mountains. It was found
in grassy pockets of soil on a rocky slope at 7,500 feet in
elevation (Correll 1944). The red spot ladies tresses
*(Schiedeella parasitica),* a fairly common but inconspicuous plant in the mountains of New Mexico, grows
only in conifer forests above 7,000 feet in the Davis and
the Guadalupe Mountains. In 1992, Kelly Bryant found
the red spot ladies tresses at an elevation of 7,500 feet
in a montane conifer forest in the Davis Mountains. It
was fairly abundant on a north-facing slope in a forest
of ponderosa and southwestern white pine. Other
prominent trees in the area included alligator juniper
*(Juniperus deppeana),* gray oak *(Quercus grisea),* and

*Hexalectris*
*grandiflora*
giant coral root

gambel oak *(Q. gambelii)* (Bryant pers. com.). This orchid has also been found recently in a montane conifer forest at an elevation of 7,800 feet in a forested canyon of the Guadalupe Mountains.

The spotted coral root *(Corallorhiza maculata)* and the striped coral root *(C. striata)* are both rare in the Trans-Pecos and grow only in a few locations. The spotted coral root was collected early in this century by E. J. Palmer in the Davis Mountains of Jeff Davis County. It was found at 7,500 feet in elevation, in rich, decaying humus in pine-hardwood forests (Correll 1944). More recently, in 1969, it was discovered at an elevation of about 5,000 feet in a deep stream bed in Juniper Canyon of the Chisos Mountains. The striped coral root *(C. striata),* with a preference for limestone soil, grows only in the Guadalupe and the Chinati Mountains. In the Guadalupe Mountains, where it is apparently quite rare, the striped coral root grows in canyon bottoms in a montane conifer forest of Douglas fir *(Pseudotsuga menziesii)* and southwestern white pine *(Pinus stroboformis)* (Brett Wauer pers. com.). The first record of this orchid in Texas is a collection from the Chinati

Mountains by West Texas botanist Leon C. Hinckley (Correll 1944).

Two inconspicuous species of *Malaxis* orchids grow in leaf mulch in woodlands and forests in the mountains of the Trans-Pecos. The mountain malaxis *(Malaxis macrostachya)* is known only from montane conifer forests on Mount Livermore in the Davis Mountains. It favors canyons and slopes near springs above 6,500 feet in elevation in a forest of ponderosa pine *(Pinus ponderosa)* and southwestern white pine *(P. strobiformis)*. Wendt's malaxis *(Malaxis wendtii)* is found only on north-facing slopes and canyons in oak-juniper-pinyon pine woodlands of the Chisos Mountains (Todsen 1995).

While other orchids in the Trans-Pecos occur only at higher elevations in the mountains, the chatterbox orchid *(Epipactis gigantea)* grows even in parched desert lowlands of the region, where it thrives in cool oases around fern-lined springs that emerge from porous limestone. It also grows at higher elevations in riparian and canyon woodlands along streams, seepages, and waterfalls.

Oak-juniper-pinyon pine woodlands are also known as pinyon pine-oak-juniper series woodlands (Diamond et al. 1987). Montane conifer forests include Douglas fir-pine series and ponderosa pine series (Diamond et al. 1987).

Orchids that grow in the Trans-Pecos must take advantage of the only rainy months of the year—July, August, and September—when much of the rainfall is associated with frequent, sometimes daily, thunderstorms. Tropical storms originating in the Gulf of Mexico or the Pacific Ocean can also bring rain in summer and early fall. Droughts, often lasting several months or more, are frequent in the Trans-Pecos. During these dry periods, orchids are scarce, and blooming and seed production are delayed until rains return and conditions are more moist.

---

**Orchids of Oak-Juniper-Pinyon Pine Woodlands in the Trans-Pecos**

*Deiregyne confusa*    Hidalgo ladies tresses
*Dichromanthus cinnabarinus*
    scarlet ladies tresses
*Epipactis gigantea*    chatterbox orchid
*Hexalectris grandiflora*    giant coral root
*H. nitida*    Glass Mountain coral root
*H. revoluta*    curly coral root
*H. spicata* var. *spicata*    crested coral root
*H. warnockii*    Texas purple spike
*Malaxis wendtii*    Wendt's malaxis
*Stenorrhynchos michuacanus*
    Michoacan ladies tresses

The rugged terrain of this area has made extensive exploration difficult. While some Texas orchid species are represented by hundreds of herbarium specimens, examples from the Trans-Pecos number only in the dozens. Traveling the harsh desert and steep canyons is made even more difficult by the weather. During the rainy season, when orchids are most likely to bloom in the area, the primitive local roads are also most likely to be washed out and impassable. In addition, many mountains in the area are on private land with limited access. Surely, more orchids will be found in the region in the future.

## THE BALCONES CANYONLANDS
### *Edge of the Edwards Plateau*

The Balcones Escarpment marks the southern and southeastern boundaries of the Edwards Plateau of Texas. The escarpment encompasses an area known as the Balcones Canyonlands, a land of steep hills and deep canyons carved by the Nueces, Frio, Sabine, Medina, Guadalupe, San Marcos, Sycamore, Pedernales, San Saba, Devil's, Colorado, and Blanco Rivers (Riskind and Diamond 1988). The region is vegetated with an odd assortment of woodland species from the deciduous forests of the eastern United States, the evergreen woodlands of northern Mexico, and the grasslands of the Great Plains (Amos and Gehlbach 1988).

In this semi-arid country, orchids can survive only in the moist canyons and riparian woodlands. Moist slopes here are wooded with Texas red oak *(Quercus buckleyi)*, plateau live oak *(Q. fusiformis)*, Ashe juniper *(Juniperus ashei)*, black cherry *(Prunus serotina)*, Texas ash *(Fraxinus texensis)*, cedar elm *(Ulmus crassifolia)*, sugarberry *(Celtis laevigata)*, netleaf hackberry *(C. reticulata)*, and Arizona walnut *(Juglans major)* (Riskind and Diamond 1988). In a few isolated areas, eastern species such as the bigtooth maple *(Acer grandidentatum)*, Carolina basswood *(Tilia caroliniana)*, and ash

(*Fraxinus* spp.) grow on moist canyon slopes and floodplains near streams. Southwestern and Mexican species such as Texas madrone *(Arbutus xalapensis)* and papershell pinyon pine *(Pinus remota)* reach their eastern limits here. Orchids of this region grow mainly in juniper-oak woodlands. This woodland type is also called Ashe juniper–oak series woodlands (Diamond et al. 1987).

The chatterbox orchid *(Epipactis gigantea),* a wide-ranging western species, is perhaps the most frequently encountered orchid in the Edwards Plateau. Here it finds refuge in secluded canyons along rocky creeks and waterfalls where springs emerge from the porous limestone of the region. In these exceedingly picturesque locations, the chatterbox orchid clings to dripping ledges, wet cliff faces, canyon walls, and stream banks, growing among lush green stands of southern shield fern *(Thelypteris kunthii)* and maidenhair fern *(Adiantum capillus-veneris).*

Four saprophytic orchids—one species of *Corallorhiza* and three species of *Hexalectris*—are found in

Waterfall at Pedernales Falls State Park, habitat of *Epipactis gigantea* chatterbox orchid

juniper-oak woodlands on bluffs, canyon slopes, and breaks on the Edwards Plateau. Here they often grow on moist north-facing and west-facing rocky slopes in the shade of large junipers and oaks. These saprophytic orchids live on deep leaf litter in well-drained, gravelly soil devoid of herbaceous ground cover. Although more abundant in East Texas, the spring coral root *(C. wisteriana)* is widespread and fairly frequent in canyon woodlands of the Edwards Plateau. The striking crested coral root *(H. spicata* var. *spicata),* although not particularly common, is widely distributed in this region. The Texas purple spike *(H. warnockii)* and the Glass Mountain coral root *(H. nitida),* once known to grow only in Trans-Pecos Texas and northern Mexico, also are found here. These elusive little orchids occur more frequently here than previously realized. They are easily overlooked in the deep shade where they reside. Apparently, many of the Glass Mountain coral roots found in this region are self-pollinated and seldom have open flowers. Bill Carr (pers. com. 1996), botanist for The Texas Nature Conservancy, found the Glass Mountain coral root in almost every juniper-oak woodland he searched on the Edwards Plateau and the adjoining Cross Timbers and Prairies region. Although less common than the Glass Mountain coral root, the Texas purple spike is also widely distributed on the Edwards Plateau. This orchid is particularly abundant on the Callahan Divide, a disjunct northern section of the Edwards Plateau consisting of a limestone ridge of steep-sided, flat-topped hills near Abilene. The Glass Mountain coral root is also found at this location, but is less numerous.

Similar juniper-oak woodlands occur in breaks on the White Rock Escarpment, a northern extension of the Balcones Escarpment, on the western edge of the Blackland Prairies (Gehlbach 1988). The spring coral root is reported from several locations on this escarpment. A few miles southwest of Dallas, the spring coral

## Orchids of Ashe Juniper–Oak Woodlands of the Balcones Canyonlands

*Corallorhiza wisteriana*   spring coral root
*Epipactis gigantea*   chatterbox orchid
*Hexalectris nitida*   Glass Mountain coral root
*H. spicata* var. *spicata*   crested coral root
*H. warnockii*   Texas purple spike
*Spiranthes cernua*   nodding ladies tresses
*S. magnicamporum*   Great Plains ladies tresses

root, the Glass Mountain coral root, the Texas purple spike, and the crested coral root all thrive in juniper-oak woodlands on this same escarpment (Engel 1987). A newly described variety of the crested coral root, *H. spicata* var. *arizonica* (Catling and Engel 1993), also occurs here.

The Great Plains ladies tresses *(Spiranthes magni-camporum)* is particularly abundant in the Balcones Canyonlands on the eastern edge of the Edwards Plateau, where it grows on gravelly limestone slopes in Ashe juniper–oak woodlands. Commonly associated with glades of grasses such as little bluestem *(Schizachyrium scoparium)* and seep muhly *(Muhlenburgia rever-chonii)*, this orchid thrives on Glen Rose limestone slopes that receive seasonal seepage water. These sites are usually wet in winter and spring, but can become excessively dry by late summer and fall. Some sites can harbor hundreds of robust flowering spikes of this fragrant orchid. It also is commonly found on moist roadbanks and in roadside ditches in this region. Although some plants bloom earlier, flowering for this frost-hardy late bloomer peaks in late November. Sometimes a few plants can still be found in bloom well into January. The nodding ladies tresses *(Spiranthes cernua)* is also reported from this region. However, the fragrant-flowered *S. magnicamporum* is almost identical in appearance to *S. cernua,* and most of the herbarium specimens labeled *S. cernua* from this limestone region may be *S. magnicamporum.* Dried herbarium specimens of these two near look-alike ladies tresses are almost impossible to distinguish (Sheviak 1982).

# TEXAS ORCHIDS BY FLOWER COLOR

The following list is designed to help you locate a species description based on the predominant color of the bloom. Most orchids have tinges of other colors in addition to their main color. The color categories below represent the predominant color in the bloom of a particular species, not necessarily the only color.

## GREEN

*Habenaria repens*    water spider orchid
*Isotria verticillata*    whorled pogonia
*Malaxis macrostachya*    mountain malaxis
*M. unifolia*    green adder's mouth
*Platanthera clavellata*    little club-spur orchid
*P. flava* var. *flava*    southern rein orchid
*P. lacera*    ragged-fringed orchid
*Tipularia discolor*    cranefly orchid

## PINK

*Calopogon oklahomensis*    Oklahoma grass pink
*C. tuberosus*    grass pink
*Cleistes bifaria*    rosebud orchid
*Deiregyne confusa*    Hidalgo ladies tresses
*Hexalectris grandiflora*    giant coral root
*Pogonia ophioglossoides*    rose pogonia

## PURPLE

*Corallorhiza maculata*    spotted coral root
*C. odontorhiza* autumn coral root

*Corallorhiza striata*    striped coral root
*C. wisteriana*    spring coral root
*Epipactis gigantea*    chatterbox orchid
*Hexalectris nitida*    Glass Mountain coral root
*H. revoluta*    curly coral root
*H. warnockii*    Texas purple spike
*Listera australis*    southern twayblade
*Malaxis wendtii*    Wendt's malaxis

## Red-Orange

*Dichromanthus cinnabarinus*    scarlet ladies tresses

## White

*Habenaria quinqueseta*    long-horned orchid
*Platanthera blephariglottis* var. *conspicua*
    white fringed orchid
*P. nivea*    snowy orchid
*Ponthieva racemosa*    shadow witch
*Schiedeella parasitica*    red spot ladies tresses
*Spiranthes brevilabris* var. *brevilabris*
    Texas ladies tresses
*S. brevilabris* var. *floridana*    Florida ladies tresses
*S. cernua*    nodding ladies tresses
*S. laciniata*    lace lip ladies tresses
*S. magnicamporum*    Great Plains ladies tresses
*S. odorata*    fragrant ladies tresses
*S. ovalis*    oval ladies tresses
*S. parksii*    Navasota ladies tresses
*S. praecox*    giant ladies tresses
*S. vernalis*    spring ladies tresses
*Stenorrhynchos michuacanus*
    Michoacan ladies tresses
*Triphora trianthophora*    three birds orchid
*Zeuxine strateumatica*    Zeuxine orchid

## Yellow

*Cypripedium kentuckiense*    southern Lady's slipper
*C. parviflorum* var. *pubescens*    yellow Lady's slipper
*Hexalectris spicata* var. *spicata*    crested coral root
*H. spicata* var. *arizonica*    Arizona crested coral root

## Yellow-Orange

*Platanthera chapmanii*   Chapman's orchid
*P. ciliaris*   yellow fringed orchid
*P. cristata*   crested fringed orchid
*P. integra*   golden frog arrow

# TEXAS ORCHIDS BY GENUS AND SPECIES

The species descriptions in this book are grouped by genus, and the genera are listed in alphabetical order (*Calopogon* through *Zeuxine*). Within each genus, the species are listed alphabetically (for example, *Spiranthes brevilabris* through *S. vernalis*).

# *Calopogon*

The genus *Calopogon* is represented by five species. One species, *C. tuberosus,* ranges throughout eastern North America from Newfoundland to Cuba and westward to Minnesota and Texas. Three species, *C. barbatus, C. multiflorus,* and *C. pallidus,* are restricted to the southeastern United States. A newly described species, *C. oklahomensis* (Goldman 1995), is confined to parts of the midwestern and southwestern United States.

Two species grow in East Texas: the grass pink *(C. tuberosus)* and the Oklahoma grass pink *(C. oklahomensis).* In Texas, *Calopogon* orchids thrive in hillside seepage bogs, wetland pine savannahs, outer edges of baygalls, moist post oak woodlands, and wet depressions in prairies. They have pink flowers with one or two grasslike leaves emerging from a fleshy, bulbous rootlike corm.

*Calopogon* flowers consist of three widespread, winglike sepals, two claw-shaped petals, and a bearded lip shaped like a fish tail and decorated by a mass of pink or white hairs with yellow tips. A long, slender, spoon-shaped column, bearing the pollen-containing anther and the stigma, projects from the center of the flower.

The genus name, *Calopogon,* combines two Greek words to mean "beautiful beard," alluding to the tufted lip. The brightly colored lip of the *Calopogon,* with numerous yellow-tipped hairs, mimics clusters of stamen laden with pollen, thus attracting bees. When a bee lights on the orchid, the hinged lip folds down onto the stigma on the column, depositing pollen brought by the bee from another grass pink orchid. When the bee departs, it grazes the anther at the tip of the column and picks up more pollen. Then, if the bee visits another orchid, the entire sequence is repeated, thus ensuring cross-pollination. (Carlyle Luer, in his monumental *Native Orchids of the United States and Canada* [1975], illustrates this process with a full page of color photographs.) The bee, a victim of the orchid's deception, receives nothing in return for its services.

## Calopogon oklahomensis

OKLAHOMA
GRASS PINK
ORCHID

*C. oklahomensis* is a newly described species from East Texas, Oklahoma, Kansas, Missouri, Arkansas, and Louisiana. *C. oklahomensis* bears two to seven fragrant flowers that are pale to deep pink. Each flower is about 1 inch in diameter, and is supported by an erect, slender stalk that can reach a height of 14 inches. The flowers of *C. oklahomensis* open in rapid succession, with several flowers appearing to bloom at once (in contrast to *C. tuberosus,* which blooms in slow succession and for a much longer period). In each flower, the fish tail–shaped lip is uppermost. The pink lip, which is about ⅗ of an inch long, has a triangular patch of short, stout hairs near its top edge with a patch of yellow ball-tipped hairs directly below. The three sepals of each flower are about ⅔ of an inch long and curve back sharply. The two oblong back-curved petals are about the same length as the sepals. The petals are broadest at the base and are tipped with a claw-shaped point. In Texas, *C. oklahomensis* occurs in damp, acidic sandy and loamy soils on the borders of wetland longleaf pine savannahs, in hillside seepage bogs, and in post oak-blackjack oak woodlands. This *Calopogon* occurs sporadically at known locations, usually appearing in abundance only after a fire. In Texas, *C. oklahomensis* blooms from late March to early May, while the much more common grass pink *(C. tuberosus)* blooms from May to July. Unlike all other species of *Calopogons,* the flower buds of *C. oklahomensis* are longitudinally grooved near the base.

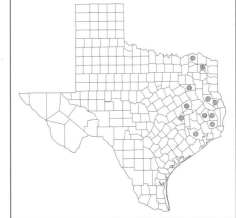

This new *Calopogon* was described by Douglas Goldman (1995), then a University of Texas graduate student conducting research on the *Calopogon* genus in North America. In the spring of 1994, Goldman visited prairie populations of *Calopogons* previously identified by botanists from Arkansas, Missouri, and Oklahoma (Summers 1987, Slaughter 1993, Magrath 1939) as a variety of *C. tuberosus.* He was surprised to find

OPPOSITE PAGE
*Calopogon
oklahomensis*
Oklahoma grass pink

these *Calopogons* unlike *C. tuberosus,* because they possessed several unique morphological and ecological characters. Goldman further observed that all small-flowered *Calopogons* from prairie sites in Oklahoma, Missouri, Kansas, and Arkansas, and from a post oak woodland in east Central Texas, shared these same characters. Goldman then examined herbarium specimens labeled as *C. barbatus* from extreme eastern Texas and western Louisiana and found that they too, although smaller in size, also possessed these same characters.

Goldman concluded that these *Calopogons* were an undescribed species. He published his findings in *Lindleyana,* the scientific journal of the American Orchid Society, and named this new species *C. oklahomensis* after the state where it was discovered and seemed to be most abundant.

The Oklahoma grass pink *(C. oklahomensis),* unlike *C. tuberosus* and *C. barbatus,* has a distinctive forked corm, widely spaced fragrant flowers, longitudinally grooved flower buds, and a leaf as long as or longer than its flowering stem. Furthermore, *C. oklahomensis* lacks the spherical white patch containing short white and orange hairs near the upper part of the lip, as displayed by *C. tuberosus,* and has a broad leaf, while *C. barbatus* has a very narrow leaf.

A specimen collected by Ferdinand J. Lindheimer in Harris County in March 1842 is perhaps the first recorded occurrence of *C. oklahomensis* in the United States (Goldman 1995). This specimen was filed away and misidentified for more than 150 years before Goldman described the new species. It represents the only known record from the Gulf Prairies and Marshes region. This rare *Calopogon* may still occur in this region of Texas, where it might be found in remnant tallgrass prairies and native grass hay meadows harvested for hay. It is currently found in coastal prairies in Jefferson Davis Parish in Louisiana.

TEXAS DISTRIBUTION
Hardin, Nacogdoches, Polk, San Augustine, and Tyler Counties in the Pineywoods; Brazos, Henderson, Lamar, Leon, and Titus Counties in the Post Oak Savannah; Harris County in the Gulf Prairies and Marshes

BLOOM TIME
March–April

GENERAL DISTRIBUTION
Arkansas, Kansas, Louisiana, Missouri, Oklahoma, Texas

BLOOM TIME
March–June

## *Calopogon tuberosus*

### Grass Pink

The grass pink orchid has from two to ten deep pink flowers, each about 1½ inches across, that bloom in a slow succession up the stem, so that the same stalk usually bears buds and open flowers simultaneously. In Texas this species blooms from early May to early July, starting nearly a month later than the smaller and much rarer Oklahoma grass pink orchid *(C. oklahomensis)*. The colorful lip, held uppermost on the flower, is

*Calopogon tuberosus*
grass pink

Rare albino form of *Calopogon tuberosus* with pure white flowers, sometimes found in the Big Thicket

bearded with yellow, orange, white, and pink ball-tipped hairs. A distinctive circular white spot that marks the heart-shaped upper portion of the lip distinguishes this species from *C.oklahomensis*. A rare albino form of *C. tuberosus* with pure white flowers is sometimes found in the Big Thicket area in the Pineywoods.

This is probably the best-known orchid in East Texas. In spring and early summer, it is a familiar sight among sphagnum moss in hillside seepage bogs, in wetland pine savannahs, and on the edges of baygalls. It also occurs, although quite rarely, in wet depressions on sandy prairies in Chambers County in the Gulf Prairies and Marshes region. The grass pink orchid thrives on moist to wet acidic sand. It often grows along with carnivorous plants such as sundew (*Drosera* spp.), butterwort *(Pinguicula pumila),* bladderwort (*Utricularia* spp.), and pitcher plant *(Sarracenia alata).* Wildflowers growing nearby may include cross-leaf milkwort

*(Polygala cruciata),* yellow savannah milkwort *(P. ramosa),* meadow beauty *(Rhexia petiolata),* pine-woods rose-gentian *(Sabatia gentianoides),* Kansas gay feather *(Liatris pycnostachya),* ten-angle pipewort *(Eriocaulon decangulare),* and Texas tickseed *(Coreopsis linifolia)* (Orzell 1990). *C. tuberosus* is pollinated by bumblebees *(Bombus* spp.) and leafcutter bees *(Megachile* spp.) (Catling and Catling 1991).

The grass pink orchid was once abundant in the wetland pine savannahs of the Big Thicket region. How-

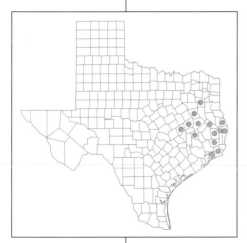

ever, many of its habitats have been destroyed by drainage, development, and the creation of pine plantations. Notable populations of the grass pink orchid are now protected in wetland pine savannahs and hillside seepage bogs in the Big Thicket National Preserve and in the Angelina National Forest (Upland Island Wilderness Area). In Angelina National Forest, the U.S. Forest Service also protects several grass pink habitats as Research Natural Areas and Botanical Areas. Long-term survival of this orchid depends on periodic fires to control invading shrubs that would eventually shade it out.

The species name, *tuberosus,* is from a Latin word meaning "swollen or tuberous," referring to the appearance of the roots. Older references refer to this species as *Calopogon pulchellus* (a Latin word for "beautiful").

Other Common Names: swamp pink, rose wings

TEXAS
DISTRIBUTION
Pineywoods, Post Oak
Savannah, and Gulf
Prairies and Marshes

BLOOM TIME
May–July

GENERAL
DISTRIBUTION
southern Ontario,
Quebec, and Newfound-
land; all states east of
the Mississippi River
and all states touching
the west bank of the
Mississippi River; Iowa,
Oklahoma, and Texas

BLOOM TIME
March–August

## Cleistes

Of the fifty-seven orchid species in the genus *Cleistes,* most occur in tropical and subtropical grassy meadows in South America. The genus name *Cleistes* is from a Greek word meaning "closed," referring to the tubular shape of the corolla, where the uppermost petals clasp the lower lip. Two species, *C. divaricata* and the smaller *C. bifaria,* are native to eastern North America, growing primarily in the wet soil of hillside seepage bogs, wetland pine savannahs, and mountain meadows. Only *C. bifaria* occurs in Texas.

It was only recently that the genus *Cleistes* in North America was separated into two distinct species, *C. divaricata* and *C. bifaria* (Catling and Gregg, 1992). M. L. Fernald first recognized the two different varieties, but Donovan Correll (1950) did not accept Fernald's varieties, so there were no further studies until that carried out by Catling and Gregg in 1992. Their study was based on measurements from 538 herbarium specimens, living populations in North Carolina, and specimens from West Virginia. Their statistical analysis of the length of column, petal, lip, and flowering stem clearly demonstrated the presence of two distinct species (*C. bifaria,* with a column length of ⅔ inch, a lip length of 1 inch, and a stem height of 14 inches; and *C. divaricata,* with a column length of 1 inch, a lip length of 1¾ inch, and a stem height of 20 inches). Other indications that these are two distinct species are their different bloom times and geographic distribution.

## Cleistes bifaria

### ROSEBUD ORCHID

The delicate pink flower of the rosebud orchid has a graceful tubular shape with a colorfully marked lip clasped in the grip of two upper petals. The lip is balanced by slender, widely spreading sepals of rich maroon. The center of the flower is hidden from view, but the tips of the upper petals curve upward to reveal a pink lip veined with purple and with a yellow ridge run-

*Cleistes bifaria*
rosebud orchid
(photographed in
southern Mississippi)

ning down the middle. The solitary flower is perched on top of a slender stem about 14 inches tall, with a single narrow leaf near the bottom of the stalk. *C. bifaria* is pollinated by bumblebees (*Bombus* spp.) and leafcutter bees (*Megachile* spp.) (Catling and Catling 1991).

In the *Flora of Texas (Orchidaceae),* Donovan Correll (1944) includes this orchid in Texas, based on one collection by E. J. Palmer. Several years before his book was published, Correll saw this specimen and recorded it in his notes, but did not note the name of the herbarium where it was housed. Finding it impossible to relocate this orchid, Correll asked Palmer, who could not recall the location where he collected the specimen. Although the orchid has not been recorded in Texas since Palmer's sighting, Correll writes that it "doubtless occurs in the southeast part" of Texas. Paul M. Catling and Katharine B. Gregg (1992) also searched in vain for the Palmer specimen, but based on information about geographic distribution, they decided that it was most likely *C. bifaria.* Apart from the Palmer sighting of this orchid, the closest sighting to Texas is from east of the Mississippi River in St. Tammany Parish, Louisiana. The rosebud orchid prefers highly acidic soils, and if it is found again in Texas, it will most likely be located in a wetland pine savannah or in a hillside seepage bog. Its dependence on fire is well known to botanists of the southeastern United States, who see it more frequently after fires.

Other Common Names: spreading pogonia, rose orchid, Lady's ettercap

TEXAS DISTRIBUTION
One record from the Pineywoods in southeast Texas

BLOOM TIME
April–May

GENERAL DISTRIBUTION
Appalachian Mountains from West Virginia to northern Georgia; North Carolina south to Florida and along the Gulf Coast to Texas

BLOOM TIME
April–July

# *Corallorhiza*

The distinctive genus *Corallorhiza,* commonly called coral root, is named for its brittle underground rhizome, a rootlike stem that resembles the branching of coral. This strange rhizome is often the same color as the plant, pinkish purple.

The genus *Corallorhiza* consists of ten saprophytic orchid species, nine of which grow only in North and Central America. (One species, *C. trifidia,* also grows in Eurasia.) Four species are native to Texas: *C. maculata, C. odontorhiza, C. striata,* and *C. wisteriana.* "A Monograph of Corallorhiza" (Freudenstein 1997) is the most current taxonomic treatment of this genus.

Because coral root orchids lack the chlorophyll necessary for photosynthesis, they rely on mycotrophism to supply the bulk of their nutrients. This always involves a symbiotic relationship with a mycorrhizal fungus capable of digesting organic debris and providing nutrients vital to the orchid.

## Corallorhiza maculata

SPOTTED
CORAL ROOT

TEXAS
DISTRIBUTION
Davis Mountains in Jeff
Davis County, Chisos
Mountains in Brewster
County in Trans-Pecos
Texas

BLOOM TIME
April–June

GENERAL
DISTRIBUTION
Newfoundland to
British Columbia; Great
Lakes states; New
England to mountains
of North Carolina,
Tennessee, and Georgia;
Texas west to Arizona
and north to Montana
and Idaho; California
north to Washington

BLOOM TIME
April–September

The spotted coral root is one of the most widespread species of *Corallorhiza*. In Texas, it is rare, growing only in the Davis and Chisos Mountains. It is more frequent in the northern coniferous forests and western mountain ranges of the United States and Canada.

It is named for the rich magenta spots that adorn the bright white lip of the flower. The lip is about ⅓ inch long and is divided into three lobes. The dorsal sepal and two petals form the top of the hooded flower. The spreading lateral sepals are colored deep crimson-purple in contrast to the bright lip. In early spring, the vivid pink shoot of the orchid pushes its way up through gravelly soil, pine needles, and oak leaves. Although the plant can grow as tall as 30 inches and bear from ten to thirty flowers, the purplish pink stem remains leafless.

The first record of the spotted coral root in Texas was a collection from the Davis Mountains by botanist E. J. Palmer. He found it in humus-rich soil in a pine-oak (montane conifer) forest at an elevation of 7,500 feet (Correll 1944). This species was found more recently along a steep stream bank in Juniper Canyon in the Chisos Mountains. Here it grows in the shade of an oak-juniper-pinyon pine woodland.

Other Common Names: many-flowered coral root, large coral root

OPPOSITE PAGE
*Corallorhiza
maculata*
spotted coral root
(photographed in
southern Colorado)

## Corallorhiza odontorhiza

AUTUMN
CORAL ROOT

The autumn coral root *(C. odontorhiza)* occurs in two different forms: a self-fertilizing (cleistogamous) type that pollinates itself within unopened flowers, and a type with open flowers pollinated by insects. The self-pollinating type is the more common of the two and is the only form that grows in Texas.

Carlyle Luer (1975) called the autumn coral root the "ugly duckling" of the colorful *Corallorhiza*.

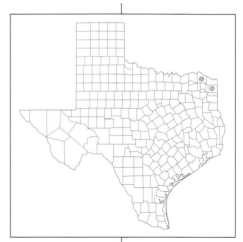

*Corallorhiza
odontorhiza*
autumn coral root

## Lone Colony Found in the Lone Star State

The autumn coral root was first discovered in northern East Texas by Geyata Ajilvsgi in a moist pine and oak forest in Cass County on September 15, 1979. On October 10, 1981, Lawrence Magrath of the University of Arts and Sciences of Oklahoma, an expert in Great Plains orchids, discovered a small colony in northeast Texas. The orchids were growing near the Oklahoma border in Red River County, on the banks of the Red River under eastern cottonwoods, sugarberry, oak, and willow.

When we visited the Red River County site in late September 1991, we did not find any of these orchids. This is not particularly surprising, because the autumn coral root is noted for its erratic appearances, seldom blooming two years in a row. E. T. Wherry believed that the root system requires several years of growth to store enough food to support even a modest bloom. After the autumn coral root blooms, the root system is often so depleted that the plant is overwhelmed by a fungus and perishes (Correll 1950). As early as 1975, Carlyle Luer published a range map indicating this orchid in Texas, but until the sightings by Ajilvsgi and Magrath, it had not been recorded with the Texas flora.

Indeed, it is the least dramatic member of the genus and the tiniest—a maximum of 8 inches tall. The closed flowers, which range in number from five to fifteen, emerge from the ends of swollen developing ovaries that are about ⅕ inch long. In turn, the ovaries are attached to the thin, brownish purple stem by means of threadlike pedicels. The sepals and petals, each about ⅕ inch long, are colored with a mixture of green suffused with purple. They converge over and enclose the white, egg-shaped lip, which is spotted with purple and approximately ⅕ inch long.

The species name, *odontorhiza*, is from a Greek word meaning "tooth root," an allusion to the white, bulbous rhizome at the base of the plant. The underground rhizome is hidden from view and, as with all native orchids, should *not* be dug up or disturbed simply for purposes of identifying it. This orchid can be positively identified by its flower characteristics and its fall blooming season.

Other Common Names: late southern coral root, fall coral root

TEXAS
DISTRIBUTION
Cass and Red River Counties in the Pineywoods; the Post Oak Savannah

BLOOM TIME
September–October

GENERAL
DISTRIBUTION
southwestern Ontario; throughout eastern United States as far north as Maine and as far south as northern Florida; all states bordering the west bank of the Mississippi River; southeastern Nebraska and South Dakota

BLOOM TIME
July–October

## *Corallorhiza striata*

### STRIPED CORAL ROOT

In Texas, *Corallorhiza striata* has been found only in the Chinati and Guadalupe Mountains.

The striped coral root is the largest and most beautiful species of genus *Corallorhiza*. The species name, *striata,* comes from Latin, meaning "striped," referring to the purplish-striped petals, sepals, and lip. The brightly striped flowers may bloom in profusion or quite scantily. The petals and sepals, each about ½ inch long, vary from yellow to pink. Each petal has five reddish purple veins, and each sepal has three. The boat-shaped, ½-inch-long lip is off-white, with broad purple veins that merge into solid purple at the tip.

This saprophytic orchid has a leafless, purple stem ranging from 4 to 20 inches tall. Three or four lighter colored sheaths conceal most of the stem.

Because the striped coral root requires cool soil temperatures, it blooms in early spring and is re-

*Corallorhiza striata*
striped coral root

TEXAS
DISTRIBUTION
Culberson and Presidio
Counties in Trans-Pecos
Texas

BLOOM TIME
May–July

GENERAL
DISTRIBUTION
New Brunswick west
to British Columbia,
dipping into the Great
Lakes states; Washing-
ton south to California;
Montana, Wyoming, and
South Dakota; Colorado,
Arizona, New Mexico,
and West Texas;
Oklahoma

BLOOM TIME
April–August

stricted to high mountains in the western states, the northern states, and Canada. It thrives in leaf mulch in densely forested canyons and on shaded stream banks, usually in calcareous and limestone soils. In Texas, it has been found only in the Chinati Mountains of Presidio County and the Guadalupe Mountains of Culberson County. In the Guadalupe Mountains, the striped coral root grows in canyon bottoms in a montane conifer forest of Douglas fir *(Pseudotsuga menziesii)* and southwestern white pine *(Pinus stroboformis)*, although it is apparently quite rare.

Other Common Name: Bigelow's coral root

*Corallorhiza wisteriana*

SPRING
CORAL ROOT

The spring coral root is the most widespread and common species of *Corallorhiza* in Texas, ranging from the Pineywoods to the Edwards Plateau.

The five to twenty-five flowers bloom as early as mid-February, making it one of the first Texas wildflowers to blossom. Each flower has three sepals and two petals that range from purplish brown to greenish yellow. The down-curved, "toothed," white lip of the flower is spotted with magenta. Several tubular sheaths of reddish brown to crimson-purple wrap around the stem, which ranges in color from purple to yellow.

Although common, this orchid, with its muted colors and tiny flowers, is seldom spotted by sheer accident; the best places to search are in leaf mulch in the shade of large trees. It can grow under a variety of trees, including pines, magnolias, beeches, oaks, and junipers. Apparently indifferent to soil moisture, it can flourish

*Corallorhiza wisteriana* spring coral root

OPPOSITE PAGE
*Corallorhiza wisteriana* is best found in leaf mulch in the shade of large trees.

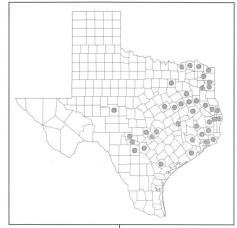

in rather dry sites as well as in moist or wet sites. The spring coral root grows most commonly on slopes and in stream terraces in pine-hardwood and floodplain forests in the Pineywoods region. It also grows rather frequently under oaks on wooded slopes on limestone bluffs, and in canyons in Ashe juniper–oak series woodlands on the Edwards Plateau and on the Austin Chalk Escarpment in the Blackland Prairies region. It grows less frequently in post oak woodlands in the Post Oak Savannah region and in live oak woodlands in the Gulf Prairies and Marshes region.

Other Common Names: Wister's coral root, early southern coral root

TEXAS
DISTRIBUTION
Pineywoods, Post Oak Savannah, Blackland Prairies, Edwards Plateau, and Gulf Prairies and Marshes

BLOOM TIME
February–March

GENERAL
DISTRIBUTION
Pennsylvania south to northern Florida and west to Arizona; Kansas west to Utah and north to South Dakota and Montana

BLOOM TIME
March–December

# *Cypripedium*

All species of *Cypripedium* are known as Lady's slippers. More than fifty species of Lady's slippers inhabit Europe, Asia, and North America.

The genus name, *Cypripedium,* combines *Kypris,* a name for Venus (who in mythology was born on Cyprus), and *pedium,* for "slipper" or "little foot," referring to the orchid's slipperlike lip. People everywhere have noticed the queenly grace of these orchids: in Italy it is called *Scarpa della Madonna* (Shoe of the Madonna), and in France it is called *Soulier de Notre Dame* (Slipper of Our Lady) and *Sabot de la Vierge* (Shoe of the Virgin).

North American yellow Lady's slippers, formerly classified as *C. calceolus* by Donovan Correll (1938), are now recognized as four closely related species included in the *C. parviflorum* complex (Sheviak 1995). Two species in this complex have been recorded in Texas: *C. parviflorum* var. *pubescens* and *C. kentuckiense.*

Field Note: In some people, the Lady's slippers cause an allergic reaction similar to that caused by poison ivy.

## *Cypripedium kentuckiense*

SOUTHERN
LADY'S
SLIPPER

The southern Lady's slipper *(C. kentuckiense),* with a 2½-inch pouchlike lip, is the largest *Cypripedium* in North America and perhaps the most spectacular orchid in Texas. Mature plants bear one to two flowers that have a pale yellow, slipperlike lip as large as an egg; a broad, leaflike dorsal sepal; and two lateral sepals that are fused together and protrude from underneath the lip. The two petals dangle to the sides like unfastened shoelaces. Petals and sepals can range from deep maroon to yellow-green with maroon mottling. The southern Lady's slipper grows to a height of about 28 inches, with three to five lancelike leaves, all about 8 inches long, that alternate up each side of the stem.

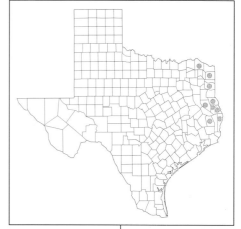

*Cypripedium
kentuckiense*
southern Lady's
slipper

*Cypripedium kentuckiense*, now rare, is usually found on terraces and lower moist slopes in pine-hardwood forests.

*C. kentuckiense* grows in only a few isolated regions in the United States: the Cumberland Plateau in Kentucky and Tennessee; the east Gulf coastal plain in Mississippi and Alabama; the Boston and Ouachita Mountains of Arkansas; and Louisiana, Oklahoma, and East Texas (Orzell and Bridges 1987). Once a frequent sight in the moist ravines of beech-dominated hardwood forests in East Texas, it is now rare. Only thirteen populations are now known in East Texas, twelve from the Pineywoods (Singhurst 1996; MacRoberts and Mac-Roberts 1997) and one from the Post Oak Savannah region (Sanders 1997). *C. kentuckiense* is currently a candidate for inclusion on the U.S. List of Endangered and Threatened Species.

This moisture-loving orchid is usually found on terraces and lower moist slopes in small stream valleys of pine-hardwood forests, where American beech *(Fagus grandiflora)*, white ash *(Fraxinus americana)*, black gum *(Nyssa sylvatica)*, and southern magnolia *(Magnolia grandiflora)* form most of the forest canopy, and where the understory is lush with flowering dogwood *(Cornus florida)*, red maple *(Acer rubrum)*, chalk maple

*(Acer leucoderma),* bigleaf snow-bell *(Styrax grandiflora),* and American hornbeam *(Carpinus caroliniana).* Two shrub species, maple-leaf viburnum *(Viburnum acerifolum)* and arrow wood viburnum *(V. dentatum),* are frequently associated with *Cypripedium kentuckiense.* Herbaceous plants commonly found near *C. kentuckiense* include another orchid species—the cranefly orchid *(Tipularia discolor)*—along with slender wood sedge *(Carex digitalis),* partridge berry *(Mitchella repens),* Christmas fern *(Polystichum acrostichoides),* Walter's violet *(Viola walteri),* eared goldenrod *(Solidago articulata),* broad beech fern *(Thelypteris hexagonoptera),* and slender wake-robin *(Trillium gracile)* (Orzell 1990).

*Cypripedium kentuckiense* was recently found in a mature shortleaf pine-oak forest in a private nature preserve in Red River County (Sanders 1997). This is the only known occurrence in the Post Oak Savannah region of East Texas.

Other Common Name: Kentucky Lady's slipper

## A Species Is Born

*Cypripedium kentuckiense* was considered by Donovan Correll (1950) to be a robust southern ecological entity of *C. calceolus* (now known as *C. parviflorum* [Sheviak 1995]). *C. kentuckiense* was declared to be a distinct species by C. F. Reed (1981) after he had examined specimens collected in Kentucky. John Atwood (1985), director of orchid research at Marie Selby Botanical Gardens in Sarasota, Florida, examined specimens from all herbaria of the southeastern United States and Texas and concluded that all Lady's slipper specimens from East Texas belonged to this new species. *C. kentuckiense* has recently been described and illustrated in *Flora of Louisiana* (1991) by Margaret Stones and Lowell Urbatsch.

TEXAS
DISTRIBUTION
Cass, Harrison, Nacogdoches, Newton, Sabine, San Augustine, Shelby, and Tyler Counties in the Pineywoods; Red River County in the Post Oak Savannah

BLOOM TIME
April

GENERAL
DISTRIBUTION
Alabama, Arkansas, Kentucky, Louisiana, Mississippi, Oklahoma, Tennessee, and East Texas

BLOOM TIME
April–May

## *Cypripedium parviflorum* var. *pubescens*

### YELLOW LADY'S SLIPPER

The yellow Lady's slipper has three to six leaves, ranging from elliptical to lance-shaped, and can grow to 24 inches tall. Each plant usually bears a single flower on a tall, slender pedicel. The flower is composed of a rich yellow, pouchlike lip up to 2 inches long and yellowish green to purplish brown petals and sepals. The slipper-like lip is often streaked or spotted with purple. The species name, *parviflorum,* means "small-flowered," a name that originally referred to the small-flowered variety of this species. (That small-flowered variety is now known as *C. parviflorum* var. *parviflorum.*) The variety name, *pubescens,* refers to the fine hairs that cover much of this large-flowered plant. The yellow Lady's slipper is pollinated by small bees (Catling and Catling 1991).

The yellow Lady's slipper grows in a variety of habitats throughout its range in colder regions of North America, including swamps, bogs, glades, rocky hillsides, and shady deciduous and

*Cypripedium parviflorum* var. *pubescens* yellow Lady's slipper (photographed in New Mexico by Tom Todsen)

coniferous woodlands. It was once collected in the Texas Panhandle near Muleshoe by B. C. Tharp (Correll 1947). This represents the only known record of this species from Texas, and it may now be extinct in the state.

Yellow Lady's slipper orchids are very widely distributed, encircling the Northern Hemisphere from North America to Europe and Asia. They occur in a baffling array of forms, which caused botanists in the early part of this century to propose many different names for the species and varieties of this perplexing group of yellow *Cypripediums*. This resulted in controversy and taxonomic uncertainty. A semblance of order was established when Donovan Correll (1938) considered all yellow Lady's slippers one polymorphic species and assigned them to *C. calceolus*. However, the North American yellow Lady's slippers are unlike the European and Asian plants, and some botanists now include them in the *C. parviflorum* complex, a distinct group of closely related North American *Cypripedium* species (Sheviak 1994). Accordingly, the large-flowered North American species that inhabits much of the eastern deciduous forests, the boreal forests and northern prairies, and the montane west should be referred to as *C. parviflorum* var. *pubescens* (Sheviak 1995).

Other Common Names: large yellow Lady's slipper, yellow moccasin flower, golden slipper, whippoorwill shoe, Noah's Ark

## Ice Age Legacy

One of the strangest discoveries of an extremely rare species in Texas was that of a yellow Lady's slipper, *Cypripedium parviflorum* var. *pubescens,* in the semi-arid Texas Panhandle (Correll 1947). In early June 1929, B. C. Tharp was exploring Bailey County near the town of Muleshoe. There, he found one Lady's slipper plant growing in a wet depression in sand dunes. Tharp described the flower's color as purplish pink, far different from the buttery yellow normal for this species.

Tharp placed the orchid specimen in the University of Texas Herbarium in Austin. When Donovan Correll (1950) examined it seventeen years later, he noted on the herbarium sheet: "doubtless yellow and purplish pink."

Tharp's specimen may have been a relict plant of the more widespread coniferous forest that once extended to lower elevations east of the Rockies during the late Pleistocene, when the climate was colder and wetter. The plant Tharp collected was possibly the last descendant of that small population. Although it is found in several locations in neighboring New Mexico, *C. parviflorum* var. *pubescens* is primarily a plant of cool northern climates. According to orchid researcher Tom Todsen of New Mexico State University, *C. parviflorum* var. *pubescens* is usually found in seeps and on north-facing slopes in coniferous forests, but never found below an elevation of 6,000 feet (Todsen pers. com. 1997).

TEXAS DISTRIBUTION
One record from the High Plains of the Texas Panhandle

BLOOM TIME
May–June

GENERAL DISTRIBUTION
Newfoundland to British Columbia and Alaska and south to Washington; New England west to North Dakota; all states east of the Mississippi River except Florida; all states touching the west bank of the Mississippi River; New Mexico and Texas

BLOOM TIME
April–July

## *Deiregyne*

The genus *Deiregyne* consists of fourteen species that are mostly native to Mexico and Guatemala (Garay 1980). One species, *D. confusa,* grows in the Chisos Mountains of Texas. Members of this genus are usually terrestrial, and have wedge-shaped leaves that narrow at the base of the leaf near the plant stalk. The leaves are usually absent when the orchid blooms. The genus name comes from two Greek words, *deire* for "neck" and *gyne* for "woman," referring to the way the sepals of the flowers rest on top of the ovary and form a slender extension like a woman's neck.

## Deiregyne confusa

### HIDALGO LADIES TRESSES

D. confusa is extremely rare in Texas. It was collected for the first and only time in Texas when J. A. Moore and J. A. Steyermark found it in the Chisos Mountains on June 22, 1931, in grassy soil pockets in rim rock at an elevation of about 7,500 feet. This specimen was labeled as *Spiranthes durangensis* (Correll 1950). According to Garay (1980) the Moore and Steyermark specimen, now housed at the Missouri Botanical Gardens, is actually *D. confusa.*

The species name, *confusa,* alludes to the fact that this species is frequently confused with the Durango ladies tresses *(D. durangensis),* which has never been documented in Texas.

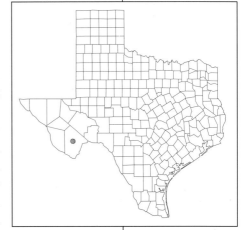

*D. confusa* has up to fifteen pale pink, green-striped flowers, each about ⅔ inch long and pointing downward. The fragrant flowers are loosely arranged along one side of the flowering stem. The dorsal sepal and two petals form a hood over a green-veined, deeply grooved whitish pink lip. The two lateral sepals point in opposite directions away from the dorsal sepal. The leafless, flowering stem sometimes reaches a height of 20 inches. *D. confusa* has two or three long, slender basal leaves that disappear before the flowers bloom.

Although this orchid is sometimes confused with *D. durangensis,* the flowers of the two species are different. In *D. durangensis,* the lip is violin-shaped and more rounded, while the lip of *D. confusa* is more slender and pointed at the tip. The sepals of *D. confusa* have swollen hairs, while the sepals of *D. durangensis* are smooth.

*D. confusa* has not been found in the United States since 1931.

TEXAS DISTRIBUTION
Chisos Mountains in Trans-Pecos Texas

BLOOM TIME
May–July

GENERAL DISTRIBUTION
Trans-Pecos Texas and Hidalgo, Mexico

BLOOM TIME
May–July

# *Dichromanthus*

This genus has only one species, *Dichromanthus cinnabarinus* (Garay 1980). This species is native to Texas, Mexico, and Guatemala. The genus name *Dichromanthus* is from the Latin *di* for "two," *chrom* for "color," and *anthus* for "flower," referring to the red and orange bloom.

*Dichromanthus
cinnabarinus*

SCARLET
LADIES
TRESSES

On a hot August day in 1883, Valery Havard discovered the first scarlet ladies tresses ever recorded in the United States (Correll 1944, 1950). He found this rare wild orchid, covered with thirty to forty large, bright red and orange blooms, growing in the foothills of the Chisos Mountains of Brewster County in what is now Big Bend National Park.

This orchid's numerous brilliant vermilion blooms and large floral bracts make it the most striking ladies tresses in Texas. The species name comes from cinnabar, a bright red orange mineral (mercuric sulfide, an ore of mercury) that was once used as a pigment. Slender petals, a lance-shaped lip, and three similarly shaped sepals form the tubular, 1-inch-long flowers. The petals, lip, and sepal curve backward at their tips, creating a wide opening at the end of the flower. The flowers are covered with fine, downy hairs, an adaptation that

*Dichromanthus
cinnabarinus*
scarlet ladies tresses

OPPOSITE PAGE
*Dichromanthus
cinnabarinus*
(scarlet ladies tresses)
was discovered growing
in the foothills of the
Chisos Mountains.

slows down the drying effects of the hot sun and low humidity.

The stout, tall plants grow from 20 to 36 inches tall and have several sheathing bracts and three to four leaves. The leaves are usually about 1½ inches wide and about 10 inches long.

These orchids grow in oak-juniper-pinyon pine woodlands on rocky, grassy slopes along intermittent stream banks or in canyons, where the fleshy roots stay moist. They often grow in the company of sotol (*Dasylirion* spp.) and lechuguilla *(Agave lechuguilla),* plants that flourish in the Chihuahuan Desert, and they usually bloom in September after the summer rains. They range widely in the mountains of Guatemala and Mexico, extending just into Trans-Pecos Texas, where they are rare, known only from Brewster County in the Chisos, Glass, and Del Norte Mountains.

While photographing the scarlet ladies tresses in the Chisos Mountains, I heard a high-pitched buzzing sound overhead, which turned out to be a hummingbird hovering just above me. It seemed to be waiting impatiently for a chance to visit this colorful orchid. The vivid vermilion tubular, horizontal flowers strongly suggest that the scarlet ladies tresses is hummingbird-pollinated (Pijl and Dodson 1966, Catling and Catling 1991).

Other Common Name: cinnabar ladies tresses

TEXAS DISTRIBUTION
Trans-Pecos Texas

BLOOM TIME
July–October

GENERAL DISTRIBUTION
Trans-Pecos Texas; Mexico; Guatemala

BLOOM TIME
July–October

# *Epipactis*

The genus *Epipactis* consists of about twenty species of orchids that mainly inhabit the temperate regions of Europe and Asia. Only one species, *E. gigantea,* commonly known as the chatterbox orchid, is native to North America. A European species, the broad-leaved helleborine orchid *(E. helleborine),* has been introduced by unknown means into eastern North America, where it seems to be an aggressive weed in some areas. Members of this genus thrive in a variety of habitats, including meadows, woodlands, swamps, and mountain ranges.

## *Epipactis gigantea*

### CHATTERBOX ORCHID

One can easily imagine being amused by the appearance of this orchid even without knowing it is commonly called the chatterbox. Its "mouth" seems to be in perpetual motion. The unusual

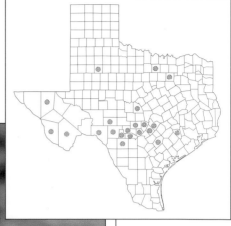

*Epipactis gigantea*
chatterbox orchid

hinged lip, when touched or stirred by a slight breeze, flaps rapidly like the jaw of an overly talkative person. The species name *gigantea* refers to the robust plants that sometimes grow more than 3 feet tall.

The flower is more than 1 inch across, with yellow-green sepals and petals, both streaked with brownish purple. The three-lobed lip is strongly veined and tinged with purple. From two to fifteen of these showy blooms may appear on one plant. Several broad, lance-shaped leaves clasp the stout stem. *E. gigantea* is pollinated by syrphid flies (Catling and Catling 1991).

The chatterbox orchid flourishes in moist gravel and sand along shady streams and waterfalls, limestone ledges, and seepage springs, mainly in the Edwards Plateau and Trans-Pecos Texas, where it often forms large colonies. It is sometimes semi-epiphytic, growing on cypress trees and on floating logs in flooded streams. Although it occasionally tolerates igneous soil, it prefers limestone soil. It frequently grows beside luxuriant stands of maidenhair fern *(Adiantum capillus-veneris)*, southern shield fern *(Thelypteris kunthii)*, and horsetail rush *(Equisetum* spp.).

Other Common Name: giant helleborine

## Chatterbox, Yes; Freeloader, No

Ferdinand Lindheimer, a German botanist who explored much of Texas around the middle of the nineteenth century, collected the chatterbox orchid *(Epipactis gigantea)* growing on a cypress tree, and mistakenly concluded that the orchid was a "parasite on the bark of baldcypress *(Taxodium distichum)*" (Correll 1944). In fact, this orchid is not parasitic, nor are the great majority of orchid species worldwide. Some orchids are epiphytic, but that simply means that they perch on trees or other plants; in fact, *epiphyte* comes from a Greek word meaning "upon plant." The word *parasite,* on the other hand, comes from a Greek word that means "one who eats at the table or at the expense of another."

TEXAS DISTRIBUTION
Primarily in the Edwards Plateau and Trans-Pecos Texas, but also reported from the Blackland Prairies, the Crosstimbers and Prairies, and the Rolling Plains

BLOOM TIME
March–August

GENERAL DISTRIBUTION
British Columbia south to California; all states west of the Rocky Mountains; Texas

BLOOM TIME
March–August

# Habenaria

*Habenaria* orchids are widespread in the tropics, with the largest concentration of species in Africa. Many *Habenaria* species grow in the Western Hemisphere, but only two occur north of Florida.

This genus once included more than five hundred species, including many species that are now classified in the genus *Platanthera.* Two *Habenaria* species have been recorded from Texas: *H. repens,* which is common and widely distributed, and *H. quinqueseta,* which has been recorded only once in Texas.

## *Habenaria quinqueseta*

### Long-Horned Orchid

The long-horned orchid was discovered in Texas in the mid-nineteenth century by Charles Wright (Correll 1944), who collected botanical specimens in Texas from 1837 to 1852 (Geiser 1948), but it has never again been recorded in the state. The species name, *quinqueseta*, is Latin for "five bristles." This refers to five long, slender appendages, three from the three-lobed lip and two from the lower lobes of each petal. The fragrant white and green flowers are about 1½ inches long. The base

*Habenaria quinqueseta* long-horned orchid (photographed in southern Georgia)

of the lip lengthens into a slender spur that grows from 2 to 4 inches long. The petals and lip are backed by a somewhat elliptical dorsal sepal and two oblong lateral sepals. The arching upper lobes of the two petals converge in front of the dorsal sepal.

A plant can grow up to 2 feet tall and bear three to fifteen flowers. The base of the stem is clasped by three to seven lancelike leaves.

This orchid was undoubtedly a rare, disjunct species in Texas when Wright collected it. It was probably an isolated occurrence at the western limit of its range. If found again in Texas, it will most likely be in a wetland pine savannah or low, wet pine-hardwood forest.

Other Common Name: Michaux's orchid

### Tracking an Anomaly

When Charles Wright made the only discovery of the long-horned orchid in Texas, he did not record the exact location. Although Donovan Correll (1950) later speculated that it was in the southeast part of the state, the location can probably be narrowed down by focusing on Wright's movements in Texas. From 1837 to 1844, he made a living primarily as a surveyor in Angelina, Jasper, Newton, and Tyler Counties, residing first in the town of Zavala, and then in Town Bluff (Geiser 1948). While working as a surveyor, he also explored intensively and collected plants. He quite likely collected the *Habenaria quinqueseta* specimen in one of these counties, which comprise the region that later became known as the Big Thicket.

TEXAS
DISTRIBUTION
Possibly Big Thicket in the Pineywoods

BLOOM TIME
April–November

GENERAL
DISTRIBUTION
North Carolina to Florida and along the Gulf Coast to Texas

BLOOM TIME
April–November

## *Habenaria repens*

### Water Spider Orchid

With its elongated spike of many green, spiderlike flowers and its watery habitat, the water spider orchid is appropriately named. The orchid's spider-legged appearance is enhanced by the lip of the flower, which is divided into three very narrow lobes, and the lateral petals, which are also divided into two thin, upward-curving lobes. The flower is about ½ inch across, with a ½- inch spur that curves downward. Leafy bracts grow under the three broad, leaflike sepals. The plant grows from 1 to 3 feet tall.

*Habenaria repens*
water spider orchid

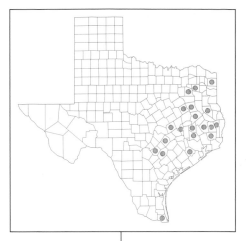

The water spider orchid can tolerate having its roots submerged for long periods, a condition that would kill most orchids. The species name *repens* means "creeping," referring to its ability to multiply by means of buds that form on the underground rhizomes. Although colonies of this orchid are rare, it can be aggressive and abundant in particular locations.

In the eastern half of Texas it is widely distributed, occurring in hillside seepage bogs, wetland pine savannahs, cypress-tupelo swamps, baygalls, ponds, ditches, and on stream banks and lake shores. On the Rio Grande Plain in South Texas, it sometimes appears in oxbow lakes (called *resacas* in that part of the country) and blooms as early as January.

Although this orchid may grow in large colonies, its green color amid the company of grasses, sedges, and rushes can make it difficult to find. In deep water, it sometimes forms floating mats of vegetation in association with other aquatic plants such as water hyacinths *(Eichhornia crassipes)*. In 1994, Kay Lewis and Frank Gregg discovered a large colony of the water spider orchids containing hundreds of plants in a small lake at Brazos Bend State Park in Fort Bend County. The sudden appearance of this orchid where it was previously unknown was quite surprising.

Other Common Name: creeping water spider orchid

TEXAS
DISTRIBUTION
Pineywoods, Post Oak
Savannah, Blackland
Prairies, and Gulf
Prairies and Marshes

BLOOM TIME
January–November

GENERAL
DISTRIBUTION
North Carolina to
Florida and along the
Gulf Coast west to Texas

BLOOM TIME
All year

# *Hexalectris*

Seven species found primarily in the mountains of northern Mexico and western Texas make up this colorful genus of saprophytic orchids. Five of those species are native to Texas, and of those five, four species grow only in the Trans-Pecos and the Edwards Plateau, Crosstimbers and Prairies, and Blackland Prairies regions. One species, *H. spicata* var. *spicata*, ranges widely from the eastern United States to Arizona and northern Mexico. The genus name *Hexalectris* literally means "six cock's combs," referring to six prominent ridges that run the length of the flower's lip at midlobe. Despite the name, most specimens have five or seven ridges on the lip, not six.

Most *Hexalectris* orchids have been described only in the last fifty years. All are exclusively mycotrophic, deriving nutrients from leaf mulch with the aid of a symbiotic fungus capable of digesting it. All species depend on an extremely delicate balance of environmental factors, making them impossible to transplant from the wild.

## Sleeping Beauties: Three Cases of Delayed Recognition

Three *Hexalectris* orchids collected in Texas were incorrectly identified, or not identified at all, for several years after their discovery. *H. revoluta*, although found in 1937, was for nine years believed to be *H. spicata* var. *spicata*, which it resembles. *H. nitida* remained in the University of Texas Herbarium from 1940 to 1946 before being recognized as a new species. *H. warnockii* was first collected in 1932, but was not formally described until eleven years after its discovery. The *Hexalectris* species descriptions provide more detail on these events.

## Hexalectris grandiflora

GIANT
CORAL ROOT

The giant coral root, with its large, pink to lavender flowers, has been considered by many, including botanist Barton Warnock, to be the most beautiful orchid in Trans-Pecos Texas. It was first discovered in the United States near Alpine in Jeff Davis County, when Mr. and Mrs. W. W. Wimberly located a population of this colorful orchid in Fern Canyon on July 7, 1925 (Correll 1944).

The bright pink, leafless plant grows anywhere from 10 to 24 inches tall, and supports as many as a dozen bright blooms nearly 1½ inches across. The flowers are a vivid pink, except for a white mark on the center of the elaborate three-lobed lip.

The giant coral root flourishes in the oak-juniper-pinyon pine woodlands of the Davis Mountains in July and August after the summer rains begin. Outside Texas, it has been reported from the mountains of north and central Mexico. It favors humus-rich soil of moist canyons, especially in the shade of oak (*Quercus* spp.) and Texas madrone *(Arbutus xalapensis)* in Texas, and bigtooth maple *(Acer grandidentatum)* and basswood *(Tilia floridana)* in northern Mexico.

Other Common Names: Greenman's hexalectris, Greenman's cock's comb

TEXAS
DISTRIBUTION
Davis Mountains in Jeff Davis County, Trans-Pecos Texas

BLOOM TIME
June–September

GENERAL
DISTRIBUTION
Trans-Pecos Texas; north and central Mexico

BLOOM TIME
May–September

OPPOSITE PAGE
*Hexalectris grandiflora*
giant coral root

## *Hexalectris nitida*

### GLASS MOUNTAIN CORAL ROOT

The blooms of the Glass Mountain coral root have a slight sheen that catches the light—hence the species name *nitida,* Latin for "glossy and polished." The spreading petals and sepals, each less than ½ inch long, are pinkish brown and veined with brown. The lip is about ½ inch long and has three lobes: the two lateral lobes are white, and the middle lobe is bright purple with five purple ridges. The thick, purple plant grows to a height of about 1 foot and supports as many as twenty blooms.

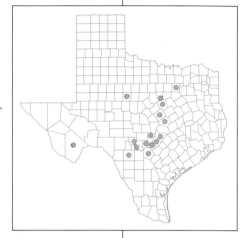

This orchid was once believed to be restricted to the Glass Mountains, but was later found both in the Chisos Mountains of Big Bend

LEFT
*Hexalectris nitida*
Glass Mountain
coral root

OPPOSITE PAGE
Closed buds on the flower stalks of *Hexalectris nitida* develop into seed capsules by self-pollination.

National Park and in the Guada-lupe Mountains. In Trans-Pecos Texas, the Glass Mountain coral root is found in moist canyons and on north-facing slopes in oak-juniper-pinyon pine woodlands. Here, it thrives on leaf litter in the shade of oak *(Quercus* spp.), Texas madrone *(Arbutus xalapensis)* and big tooth maple *(Acer grandidentatum)*. In 1975, it was discovered in Abilene State Park on the Callahan Divide, a northern extension of the Edwards Plateau. Since that time, it has been found in several other locations on the Edwards Plateau, where it favors juniper-oak woodlands and sometimes grows near the Texas purple spike orchid *(Hexalectris warnockii)*.

Most of the *H. nitida* orchids that grow on the Edwards Plateau appear to be self-pollinating, or cleistogamous, and only occasionally display open flowers. The term *cleistogamous* is Latin for "a closed union," referring to self-pollinated flowers that remain closed. The flower stalk bears tightly closed buds that develop into seed capsules by self-pollination.

Other Common Name: shining cock's comb

## Prize on Panther Hill

Texas botanist Barton Warnock discovered a new species, the rare Glass Mountain coral root, on August 2, 1940. Warnock, then a graduate student at the University of Texas, was studying the vegetation of the Glass Mountains for his Ph.D. dissertation.

While exploring a shaded canyon on Panther Hill, he found this orchid at the base of a boulder pile. In 1946, six years after Warnock's discovery, Donovan Correll (1950) examined this specimen and recognized it as a species described by Louis Otho Williams in 1944. Williams based his description on a specimen that was collected in the state of Coahuila, Mexico, in 1941.

TEXAS DISTRIBUTION
Brewster and Pecos Counties in Trans-Pecos Texas; Bandera, Bexar, Blanco, Comal, Hays, Kendall, Kerr, Real, Taylor, and Travis Counties on the Edwards Plateau; Bosque, Coryell, and Somervell Counties in the Cross Timbers and Prairies; Dallas County in the Blackland Prairies

BLOOM TIME
June–August

GENERAL DISTRIBUTION
Texas; Carlsbad, New Mexico; Coahuila, Mexico

BLOOM TIME
June–August

## *Hexalectris revoluta*

### Curly Coral Root

**Big Bend Bonanza**

In 1937, Barton Warnock, who was then an undergraduate student at Sul Ross State University at Alpine, spent much of the summer exploring and collecting plants from the Chisos Mountains in the largely uncharted Texas Canyonlands State Park, now Big Bend National Park. On July 16, while prospecting along Willow Creek in the basin area of the Chisos Mountains, he discovered the first *Hexalectris revoluta* in the United States. At that time, however, the specimen was wrongly identified as *H. spicata* var. *spicata* because of its similar appearance.

For the next nine years, Warnock's specimen remained filed away at the Sul Ross State University Herbarium until Donovan Correll (1950) correctly identified it as *H. revoluta*. Correll was quite familiar with *H. revoluta*, having authored the species description five years earlier. Correll wrote his description based on a specimen collected in 1934 by C. H. and M. T. Muller in Nuevo León, Mexico.

The bloom of the curly coral root is about 1 inch wide, and is purplish tan with darker veins. The lip of the flower is deeply divided into three lobes. The white lateral lobes are marked with crimson veins, and the bright purple middle lobe, fluted at the edge, has three white ridges. The shape of the sepals and petals is suggested by the species name, *revoluta,* which comes from a Latin word that means "rolled back."

About fifteen flowers are widely spaced on the 12-inch to 18-inch stalk. Several short purple sheaths clasp the stem.

The curly coral root is saprophytic, living on decayed matter in moist and dry oak-juniper-pinyon pine woodlands of rocky streams and canyons. Although it usually blooms in June and July, it sometimes blooms as early as May when spring rains are abundant. In the Chisos Mountains, it sprouts in the rich humus under oak trees, usually the Graves oak *(Quercus gravesii)*. In the Glass Mountains, it grows along with *Hexalectris nitida* in shady spots under lechuguilla *(Agave lechuguilla)* and under shinnery oak *(Quercus mohriana)* on sunny slopes and ridges (Warnock 1977).

Only six populations of this orchid have been recorded, all of them in Texas and northern Mexico.

Other Common Name: Correll's cock's comb

TEXAS DISTRIBUTION
Chisos and Glass Mountains in Brewster County, Guadalupe Mountains in Culberson County in Trans-Pecos Texas

BLOOM TIME
May–August

GENERAL DISTRIBUTION
Trans-Pecos Texas; Nuevo León and San Luis Potosí, Mexico

BLOOM TIME
May–August

**Hexalectris spicata var. spicata**

CRESTED
CORAL ROOT

The brightly colored, even lurid, flowers of the crested coral root grow on a tall, leafless stalk of fleshy pink. The flower's creamy yellow petals and sepals are beautifully striped with brownish purple, and the ornate white lip is adorned with five to seven wavy crests of deep purple. Several sheathlike bracts are widely spaced on the stem of the plant, which may bear up to twenty-five blooms.

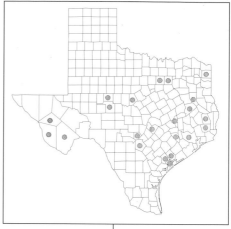

The crested coral root is the most widely distributed member of the genus *Hexalectris,* ranging along the Atlantic Coast and Gulf Coast and extending as far west as Arizona and as far south as Mexico. It thrives in leaf mold in the deep shade of hardwoods and conifers on well-drained knolls and stream banks, and has been found growing on rotting logs. Although known to prefer limestone soils, it sometimes

*Hexalectris spicata* var. *spicata* grows in leaf mold in the deep shade of hardwoods and conifers.

*Hexalectris spicata*
var. *spicata*
crested coral root

grows in mineral-rich, slightly acidic soil. In Texas, the crested coral root is uncommon. It is most frequent on wooded limestone hillsides and canyon slopes in juniper-oak woodlands of the Edwards Plateau. It is also found sparingly in similar woodland habitats in the Crosstimbers and Prairies and in the Blackland Prairies regions. It is occasionally found in post oak woodlands of the Post Oak Savannah region, pine-hardwood forests in the Pineywoods region, and coastal live oak woodlands in the Gulf Prairies and Marshes region. Although rare, it also grows in oak-juniper-pinyon pine woodlands in the mountains of Trans-Pecos Texas.

Other Common Names: cock's comb, brunetta

TEXAS
DISTRIBUTION
Widespread

BLOOM TIME
April–August

GENERAL
DISTRIBUTION
Maryland and West Virginia, along the Atlantic Coast into Florida, and west to Arizona; throughout all Deep South states; Kentucky, Missouri, Arkansas; Mexico

BLOOM TIME
April–August

## *Hexalectris spicata* var. *arizonica*

ARIZONA
CRESTED
CORAL ROOT

*H. spicata* var. *arizonica,* a new variety of *H. spicata,* was recently described in *Lindleyana,* the scientific journal of the American Orchid Society (Catling & Engel 1993).

This rare variety, much less attractive than *H. spicata* var. *spicata,* has smaller, pale creamy yellow to pinkish flowers that almost never open fully. The creamy yellow to pinkish petals and sepals, striped with purple, converge at their tips to form the somewhat closed flower. Partially concealed by the petals and sepals, the

*Hexalectris spicata* var. *arizonica* Arizona crested coral root

three-lobed lip is veined with purple and bears five crests.

Flowers of this variety lack a rostellum, a structure on the column that separates the anther from the stigma and prevents self-pollination in cross-pollinating orchids. It is cleistogamous, which literally means "self-pollinating with closed flowers." The vast majority of plants of this variety have closed flowers, but some plants with open flowers occasionally occur. This new variety was discovered in an oak-juniper woodland in southwestern Dallas County by Dale Williams and Victor Engel in 1982 (Catling and Engel 1993). Three other members of the *Hexalectris* genus also grow at this site: *H. nitida, H. warnockii,* and *H. spicata* var. *spicata.*

Williams and Engel had observed this closed-flowered form of *H. spicata* for several years and considered it a hybrid between *H. spicata* and *H. nitida.* This odd *Hexalectris* orchid also attracted the attention of Canadian orchidologist Paul Catling, who determined there was insufficient evidence of pollen or seed sterility to indicate hybridization. Therefore, Catling proposed the varietal rank *H. spicata* var. *arizonica* for this closed-flowered orchid. The varietal name *arizonica* is named after the state of Arizona, where the first known herbarium specimen was collected in 1882 by S. Watson (Catling and Engel 1993). *H. spicata* var. *arizonica* is a geographically restricted orchid, occurring only in Arizona, Texas, and Coahuila, Mexico.

TEXAS DISTRIBUTION
Anderson County in the Pineywoods; Brewster and Culberson Counties in Trans-Pecos Texas; Dallas County in the Blackland Prairies; Travis County in the Edwards Plateau; Palo Pinto County in the Crosstimbers and Prairies

BLOOM TIME
May–August

GENERAL DISTRIBUTION
Arizona; Texas; Coahuila, Mexico

BLOOM TIME
May–August

## Hexalectris warnockii

### TEXAS PURPLE SPIKE

The slender, reddish purple stems of the Texas purple spike orchid support as many as ten large, drooping maroon flowers, each about 1 inch wide. The multicolored lip of the flower protrudes from underneath the widely spreading, waxy, maroon sepals and petals. The lip is divided into two lateral lobes, veined in reddish purple, and a white middle lobe. The middle lobe is adorned with five bright yellow-orange, waxy crests and a blotch of purple at the apex.

This is the most common *Hexalectris* in the Chisos Mountains of Big Bend National Park, appearing every year when there is enough rainfall. It also grows in other mountains of Trans-Pecos Texas and is fairly widespread in the Edwards Plateau. It has been found as far north as the Callahan Divide south of Abilene and the White Rock (Austin Chalk) Escarpment south of Dallas.

In the mountains of Trans-Pecos Texas, *H. warnockii* is found on shaded slopes and dry, rocky creek beds. It grows in leaf mulch under oak, madrone, and pinyon

### Barton Warnock: The Wizard of Orchids

It is nearly impossible to discuss the flora of West Texas without mentioning Dr. Barton Warnock, who was an authority on plants of Trans-Pecos Texas and author of three books and many articles on Texas wildflowers. His books include *Wildflowers of the Davis Mountains and Marathon Basin* (1977), *Wildflowers of the Guadalupe Mountains and the Sand Dune Country* (1974), and *Wildflowers of the Big Bend Country* (1970).

Warnock discovered *Hexalectris revoluta* in 1937 and *H. nitida* in 1940. When the Texas purple spike orchid was named *H. warnockii* in his honor, it was also described using a specimen he collected in 1937. At least twelve species of plants were named for him. The plants he collected over many decades comprise the bulk of the specimens in the herbarium at Sul Ross State University at Alpine, where he served as professor of biology.

Even late in his life, Dr. Warnock actively explored the mountains of Trans-Pecos Texas in search of new species, sometimes with the aid of a helicopter to reach particularly inaccessible sites. He planted and maintained a renowned garden on Iron Mountain near Marathon that showcased Texas wildflowers, cacti, and shrubs. Always willing to share his knowledge and appreciation of the native Texas flora, he conducted tours of the garden by appointment, generously shared information with younger botanists, and participated actively in educational and conservation projects of the Big Bend Natural History Association.

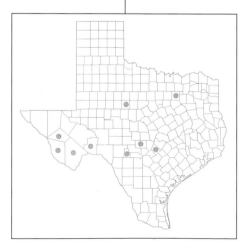

OPPOSITE PAGE
*Hexalectris warnockii*
Texas purple spike

pine in oak-juniper-pinyon pine woodlands. In the Edwards Plateau, it favors rocky limestone soils covered with leaf mulch in juniper-oak woodlands.

The Texas purple spike orchid was thought to be restricted to Trans-Pecos Texas until 1946, when Helen Correll (Correll 1950) located a specimen in Gillespie County on the Edwards Plateau. This orchid is now known to occur in several locations on the Edwards Plateau and in a few sites on the Austin Chalk Escarpment in the Blackland Prairies region.

Other Common Names: None known

### Saga of an Unknown Species

The Texas purple spike orchid was not recognized as a new species until more than a decade after its discovery. On July 20, 1932, University of California botanist C. H. Muller first collected it in Love Peak Basin in the Chisos Mountains.

The orchid was finally described and named eleven years later; however, the description was not based on the specimen Muller collected, but on one collected by Barton Warnock on June 25, 1937, from Upper Blue Creek Canyon in the Chisos Mountains. Botanists Oakes Ames and Donovan Correll, who described the species and named it in honor of Warnock, were also well known in the field of orchidology.

TEXAS
DISTRIBUTION
Brewster, Jeff Davis, Presidio, Real, and Terrell Counties in Trans-Pecos Texas; Gillespie, Hayes, and Taylor Counties in the Edwards Plateau; Dallas County in the Blackland Prairies

BLOOM TIME
June–September

GENERAL
DISTRIBUTION
Texas; southeast Arizona; Baja California, Mexico

BLOOM TIME
September

# *Isotria*

The genus *Isotria* is comprised of two species, *I. verticillata* and *I. medioloides,* that grow throughout the eastern United States. Of these two, only *I. verticillata,* the larger and more common species, is found in Texas. *Isotria,* the genus name, combines two Greek words that mean "equal" and "three," referring to the three almost identical sepals that are equal in length.

## Isotria verticillata

WHORLED POGONIA

The rare whorled pogonia has a large, unusual flower with three long, narrow, widely spreading brownish purple sepals. The narrow, 1-inch-long yellow-green lip is lined with purple and crested with a fleshy ridge. The yellowish green lateral petals overlap and enclose the lip, forming a tubular corolla.

*Isotria verticillata*
whorled pogonia

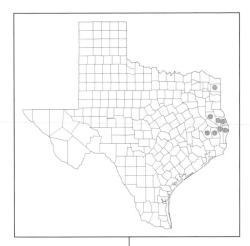

The hollow stem is topped with five or six pointed, oblong leaves arranged in a pattern suggested by the species name *verticillata*, meaning "whorled" in Latin. Soon after the leaves appear in early spring, the flower blooms. As the seedpod develops, the leaves continue to expand to four or five times their original size. The willowy, fibrous roots run horizontally underground and can be several feet long. *I. verticillata* is pollinated by small bees, including andrenid bees (Andrenidae), green metallic bees (Halictidae), and digger bees (Anthophoridae) (Catling and Catling 1991).

The whorled pogonia prefers acid soil and inhabits slopes and stream terraces in the moist, sandy, pine-hardwood forests of East Texas. It often appears on the margins of baygalls, growing with royal fern *(Osmunda regalis)* and cinnamon fern *(O. cinnamonea)*.

Other Common Names: large whorled pogonia, five-leaves orchid

TEXAS DISTRIBUTION
Cass, Jasper, Nacogdoches, Newton, Polk, Sabine, San Augustine, and Tyler Counties in the Pineywoods

BLOOM TIME
March–April

GENERAL DISTRIBUTION
eastern United States ranging from Maine south to Florida, west to Texas, and north to Michigan

BLOOM TIME
March–August

## Listera

*Listera,* the twayblade orchids, are named for Dr. Martin Lister (1638–1711), a pioneer paleontologist, physician, and English naturalist. The genus *Listera* includes twenty-five orchid species that grow in cool, temperate regions of the Northern and Southern Hemispheres.

Commonly know as twayblade orchids, all members of this genus are small and inconspicuous, with only two opposing leaves near the middle of the stem.

## *Listera australis*

### SOUTHERN TWAYBLADE

The diminutive southern twayblade orchid, 6 inches tall at most, can be difficult to spot in the shade of the moist, rich forests it favors. The five to twenty-five widely spaced, reddish purple flowers have a deeply divided, two-pronged lip about ½ inch long. Two opposing tiny leaves, egg-shaped except for a point on the end, occur midway up the purplish green stem.

This orchid sends up leaves in late winter, sometimes blooming as early as February 1. Soon after the flowers are pollinated, the seedpods ripen. This strategy allows the plants to grow in the abundant sunlight of late winter and early spring, before the forest canopy is in full leaf.

Although the southern twayblade orchid is common, it is so inconspicuous that it was once believed to be very rare. Donovan Correll (1950) listed it as growing

*Listera australis*
southern twayblade

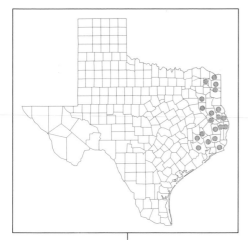

in only three counties in the southeastern corner of Texas, namely Harris, Hardin, and Jefferson. Today, it is known to grow throughout the Pineywoods region of East Texas. The species name *australis* means "southern," but this orchid has been found as far north as Canada. In Texas, the southern twayblade orchid occurs along streams and ravines in low, moist pine-hardwood forests, and often grows on clumps of moss in rich humus and leaf litter. It is particularly abundant in beech-dominated pine-hardwood forests.

Other Common Name: long-lip twayblade

**TEXAS DISTRIBUTION**
Pineywoods

**BLOOM TIME**
February–March

**GENERAL DISTRIBUTION**
Nova Scotia, southern Quebec; Vermont, New York, New Jersey; Virginia south to Florida and west to Texas; Arkansas and Tennessee

**BLOOM TIME**
January–July

OPPOSITE PAGE
The common *Listera australis* can be difficult to spot.

# Malaxis

The genus *Malaxis* is represented by nearly two hundred species worldwide, occurring on every continent except Africa. *Malaxis* is Greek for "soft," alluding to the tender, fleshy leaves of some orchids in this genus. Three *Malaxis* orchids are native to Texas: *M. wendtii* and *M. macrostachya* from the mountains of Trans-Pecos Texas, and *M. unifolia* from the Pineywoods of East Texas.

## *Malaxis macrostachya*

### MOUNTAIN MALAXIS

The mountain malaxis orchid has many tiny flowers and a single vertical leaf. The flowers are scarcely ¹⁄₁₀ inch across and are often highly variable in shape, even on the same spike. From a short distance, the flower-covered stalk resembles the rough, rubbery tail of a rat, giving rise to its other common name, the rattail malaxis. The species name *macrostachya* means "large spike" in

*Malaxis macrostachya*
mountain malaxis

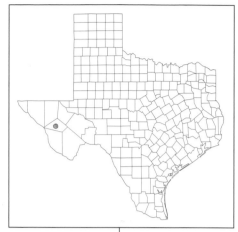

Greek, alluding to the appearance of the spike when it is covered with blooms.

This orchid ranges from Central America to northern Mexico, Arizona, New Mexico, and West Texas. It generally occurs at high elevations on rocky slopes of moist canyons in mixed conifer and hardwood forests (Correll 1950). In Texas, the mountain malaxis is found only in the Davis Mountains of Trans-Pecos Texas. Here, this orchid grows in leaf mulch in moist forested canyons from 6,500 to 7,500 feet in elevation. It favors rocky slopes near springs in montane conifer forests of ponderosa *(Pinus ponderosa)* and southwestern white pine *(Pinus strobiformis)*.

Other Common Name: rattail malaxis

TEXAS DISTRIBUTION
Trans-Pecos Texas

BLOOM TIME
July–October

GENERAL DISTRIBUTION
Texas, New Mexico, Arizona, Mexico, Central America

BLOOM TIME
July–October

## *Malaxis unifolia*

### Green Adder's Mouth

The green adder's mouth orchid is named for two fanglike, pointed lobes of the flower's lip. The tiny green flowers are densely packed at the top of the stem, giving the plant as a whole a flat-topped appearance. Although the plant can grow up to 18 inches tall, its overall greenness and tiny flowers make it easy to overlook, so it may be more common than is realized.

The single, bright green leaf (alluded to in the species name, *unifolia*) sheaths the lower portion of the stem and expands abruptly about midway up the stem. The leaf is about 2 to 3 inches wide near its base and tapers almost to a point at its tip.

In the Pineywoods of East Texas, this orchid prefers moist, forested slopes along streams in pine-hardwood forests. Its favored spots are often around the edges of baygalls.

Other Common Name: green malaxis

*Malaxis unifolia*
green adder's mouth

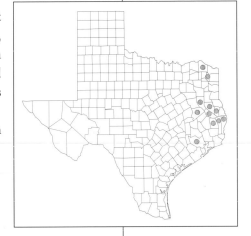

TEXAS
DISTRIBUTION
Pineywoods

BLOOM TIME
May–June

GENERAL
DISTRIBUTION
Newfoundland west to Manitoba; all states east of the Mississippi River and all states touching the west bank of the Mississippi River; Texas

BLOOM TIME
February–August

## Malaxis wendtii

### WENDT'S MALAXIS

*M. wendtii* has a long, feathery flowering stem clasped by a solitary green leaf. It can bear as many as sixty tiny purple blooms. Each minute, velvety purple flower is less than ¼ inch wide and has a narrow, arrow-shaped lip, two slender, spreading petals, and three elliptical sepals. The microscopic column is about .02 inches wide and projects from the center of the flower. This orchid was formerly known as *Malaxis ehrenbergii,* but recent research indicates that it is *Malaxis wendtii,* a newly named species (Salazar 1993, Todsen 1995). Microscopic, nipple-shaped hairs on the upper surfaces of the sepals, petals, and lip distinguish this orchid from other species.

*M. wendtii* is named for botanist Tom Wendt, who collected the type specimen used to describe this species. His collections and writings also contributed much new information to the flora of several regions of Mexico.

*Malaxis wendtii* grows in leaf mold on rocky slopes that face north and west in oak-coniferous forests, and among submontane shrub vegetation at 5,600 to 9,000 feet in elevation in northern Mexico (Salazar 1993). In Texas, it is known to inhabit moist canyons and north-facing slopes in oak-juniper-pinyon pine woodlands of the Chisos Mountains in Big Bend National Park (Todsen 1995).

Other Common Names: None known

TEXAS
DISTRIBUTION
Chisos Mountains in Trans-Pecos Texas

BLOOM TIME
July–September

GENERAL
DISTRIBUTION
Trans-Pecos Texas to New Mexico and Arizona; Coahuila and Nuevo León, Mexico

BLOOM TIME
July–September

OPPOSITE PAGE
*Malaxis wendtii*
Wendt's malaxis

## Platanthera

The genus *Platanthera*, meaning "broad anther," is represented in Texas by nine species. *Platanthera* orchids are considered by many orchidologists, including Oakes Ames (1924) and Donovan Correll (1950), to be part of the genus *Habenaria*. However, other botanists have divided *Habenaria* into several genera, based on morphological characteristics that are often quite variable.

Carlyle Luer (1975) found several good reasons to separate *Platanthera* from *Habenaria*. *Platanthera* orchids grow in the Northern Hemisphere in North America, Europe, and Asia. *Habenaria* orchids grow primarily in the tropics, with only two species of the entire genus found north of Florida. Further, the roots of *Habenaria* have bulblike tubers; in contrast, the roots of *Platanthera* usually lack this feature. Also, the lip and the petals of *Platanthera* are usually not divided into multiple linear parts as in most *Habenaria*. Finally, *Habenaria* orchids have a distinctive pair of fleshy projections from the stigma, at or below the entrance to the nectary, while *Platanthera* species do not.

## *Platanthera blephariglottis* var. *conspicua*

### White Fringed Orchid

The profusely blooming raceme of flowers is easily distinguished by its ½-inch-long fringed, white lips, alluded to in the species name *blephariglottis*, which means "fringed tongue." The variety *conspicua* designates the more robust southern form of *P. blephariglottis*. Except for its white flower and its more coarsely fringed lip, this orchid is almost identical to the yellow fringed orchid *(P. ciliaris)*. The thick-stemmed plant can reach a height of more than 3 feet, and usually has from two to

*Platanthera blephariglottis* var. *conspicua* white fringed orchid (photographed in northern Florida)

four long, slender leaves. *P. blephariglottis* var. *conspicua* is pollinated by sphinx moths, butterflies, and sometimes bumblebees (Catling and Catling 1991).

In Texas, this orchid has been collected only from Galveston County in the Gulf Prairies and Marshes region of southeast Texas. The white fringed orchid *(P. blephariglottis* var. *conspicua)* was collected for the first and only time in Texas by L. R. Moyer in the early 1900s (Correll 1944). Donovan Correll (1950) considered the Galveston County site, which was then the only known record west of the state of Mississippi, a "probable disjunct station." The typical habitats for this uncommon orchid are wetland pine savannahs, hillside seepage bogs, and the sunny edges of baygalls. In these habitats, it grows in wet, acidic, sandy, organic-rich muck and sphagnum moss. The white fringed orchid also grows in freshwater marshes. Most likely, Moyer collected *P. blephariglottis* var. *conspicua* from a freshwater marsh, since other habitats preferred by this orchid are not known in Galveston County. The white fringed orchid was discovered in eastern Louisiana for the first time in 1985 in St. Tammany Parish (Stones and Urbatsch 1991). More recently, a small population was reported near Leesville, Louisiana, in Vernon Parish, fewer than 50 miles from the Texas border (MacRoberts and MacRoberts 1995).

Other Common Name: plume of Navarre

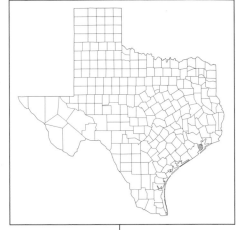

TEXAS
DISTRIBUTION
One collection from
Galveston County in the
Gulf Prairies and
Marshes

BLOOM TIME
August–September

GENERAL
DISTRIBUTION
Newfoundland; New
England, New York west
to Michigan; New Jersey
south to Florida; Deep
South states west to
Texas; Illinois

BLOOM TIME
June–October

## *Platanthera chapmanii*

### Chapman's Orchid

Sixty or more bright orange blooms are densely packed into a cylindrical raceme on the slender stem of Chapman's orchid. This extravagance of orange blooms makes it look much like *P. cristata*, but the flowers of *P. cristata* are considerably smaller. *P. chapmanii* is also sometimes confused with a species that has larger blooms, *P. ciliaris*. Chapman's orchid has a distinctive spur about the same length as the ovary-containing pedicel. The lip of the flower is ⅓ inch long, and the plant can reach a height of about 3 feet. The plant bears two long, slender leaves and several leaflike bracts. *P. chapmanii* is pollinated by large butterflies, primarily swallowtails (Catling and Catling 1991).

Orchidologist Oakes Ames (1910) (and many botanists who followed him) believed that *P. chapmanii* was a hybrid between *P. ciliaris* and *P. cristata*. Today, however, *P. chapmanii* is considered a distinct species (Folsom 1984). It was first collected in 1868 in northern Florida by Dr. Saurman and again in 1882 by A. W. Chapman, for whom it is named (Luer 1975). *P. chapmanii* is a rare, geographically restricted orchid, found only in southeastern Georgia, northern Florida, and southeastern Texas.

Although never widespread, populations of *P. chapmanii* were once locally abundant in the Big Thicket, especially in wetland pine savannahs near the town of War-

### Separate Species or "Missing Link"?

*Platanthera chapmanii* was first described by J. K. Small in *Flora of the Southeastern United States* (1903), using a specimen collected from Apalachicola, Florida. Small named the species after the botanist who collected the specimen, A. W. Chapman. Oakes Ames, however, did not agree with Small's classification. Because *P. chapmanii* is intermediate in size and floral morphology to *P. ciliaris* and *P. cristata,* Ames believed this orchid to be a hybrid of these two species, and named it *P. x chapmanii*.

Agreeing with Small, James Folsom (1984) considered *P. chapmanii* a separate species because it grows true from seed, has its own unique pollination mechanism, occurs in populations isolated from *P. ciliaris* and *P. cristata,* and has a distinctive bent column, unlike *P. ciliaris* and *P. cristata*. In addition, most populations of *P. chapmanii, P. ciliaris,* and *P. cristata* in the southeastern United States grow in pure stands with no intermediates or hybrids. Hybrids between *P. ciliaris* and *P. cristata* do occur in nature, but they are exceedingly rare. These hybrids lack the distinctively bent column that distinguishes *P. chapmanii*.

Near Apalachicola, Florida, where *P. chapmanii* is found, populations of *P. ciliaris* are unexpectedly absent, even though *P. ciliaris* is common elsewhere in northern Florida. In Texas, *P. chapmanii* occurs in Hardin, Orange, and southern Tyler Counties; but as in Florida, *P. ciliaris,* although somewhat common in other areas of southeast Texas, is never found in the same areas as *P. chapmanii*.

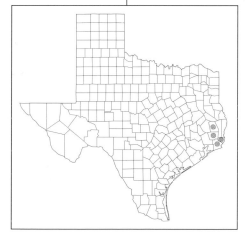

ren in southern Tyler County. Recently, residential and pine-plantation development has destroyed most of the habitat of this orchid in southeast Texas, but it can still be found in a few spots in the Big Thicket of East Texas. In those sites, this acid-loving orchid thrives in sphagnum moss in flat wetland pine savannahs.

*Platanthera*
*chapmanii*
Chapman's orchid

TEXAS
DISTRIBUTION
Hardin, Jefferson,
Orange, and Tyler
Counties in the
Pineywoods

BLOOM TIME
July–August

GENERAL
DISTRIBUTION
southeastern Georgia;
northern Florida;
eastern Texas

BLOOM TIME
July–August

## *Platanthera ciliaris*

### Yellow Fringed Orchid

The yellow fringed orchid, which produces as many as thirty to sixty large, bright orange flowers and grows up to 3 feet high, is the showiest and best known *Platanthera* orchid in Texas. The flower resembles the head of an alien creature in a science-fiction movie, with a helmet-shaped dorsal sepal and two large, earlike lateral sepals. The column, with its mouth-shaped open-

*Platanthera ciliaris*
yellow fringed orchid

ing, and the spur and rounded knobs on the sides of the anther, complete the strange "face." A ½-inch-long fringed lip looks like a beard; in fact, the species name *ciliaris* is Latin for "fringed with hairs."

The thin spur of the lip, up to 1⅓ inches long, is much longer than the pedicel, a characteristic that distinguishes *ciliaris* from other orange orchids of the genus *Platanthera*. Two to four long, slender, shiny green leaves clasp the lower portion of the stem, and several leaflike bracts protrude from the upper portion of the stem. *P. ciliaris* is pollinated by large butterflies, primarily swallowtails (Catling and Catling 1991).

Although the yellow fringed orchid occurs as far west as Milam County in Texas, it is mostly restricted to the Pineywoods region of East Texas. It thrives in the acid soil of hillside seepage bogs and baygalls, where it tolerates light levels that range from full sun to partial shade. It grows in the company of sphagnum moss, royal fern *(Osmunda regalis* var. *spectabilis),* and cinnamon fern *(O. cinnamonea).* The yellow fringed orchid is by far the most common summer-blooming orchid in East Texas.

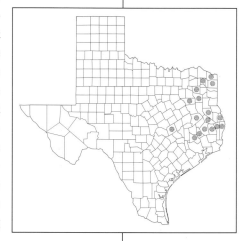

Other Common Name: orange plume orchid

TEXAS
DISTRIBUTION
Pineywoods and Post
Oak Savannah

BLOOM TIME
July–August

GENERAL
DISTRIBUTION
southern Ontario; all
states east of the
Mississippi River as far
north as Massachusetts;
Missouri south to
Louisiana and Texas

BLOOM TIME
July–September

## *Platanthera clavellata*

### Little Club-Spur Orchid

When in bloom, the little club-spur orchid is not likely to be confused with any other *Platanthera* orchid. Three to fifteen tiny greenish white flowers twist about 45 degrees away from the vertical axis of the stem, making them look somewhat askew. *Clavellata,* the species name, refers to the club-shaped appearance of spurs on the flowers. This orchid can reach a height of 4 to 12 inches, and has one oblong leaf and a few leaflike bracts.

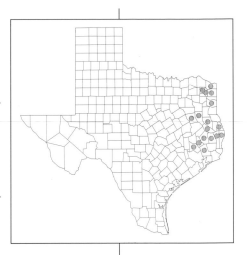

*Platanthera clavellata*
little club-spur orchid

TEXAS
DISTRIBUTION
Pineywoods

BLOOM TIME
June–July

GENERAL
DISTRIBUTION
Newfoundland to
Ontario; all states east
of the Mississippi River
and all states touching
the west bank of the
Mississippi River; Texas;
Oklahoma

BLOOM TIME
June–September

Although it can grow in sunny or shady bogs and swamps of the northern United States, in the South it lives only in shade. In Texas, it favors mucky saturated soils along stream banks and standing water in baygalls. It often grows under a canopy of sweetbay magnolia *(Magnolia virginiana)*, red bay *(Persea palustris)*, and black gum *(Nyssa sylvatica* var. *biflora)*, in the company of bristle-stalked sedge *(Carex leptalea)*, sphagnum moss, royal fern *(Osmunda regalis* var. *spectabilis)*, Virginia chain fern *(Woodwardia virginica)*, and cinnamon fern *(Osmunda cinnamonea)*.

Other Common Names: green wood orchid, small green wood orchid, wood orchid

*Platanthera clavellata* grows with sedges, sphagnum moss, and ferns in saturated soils of the Pineywoods.

## *Platanthera cristata*

CRESTED
FRINGED
ORCHID

The crested fringed orchid has small flowers that resemble miniature versions of yellow fringed orchid blooms *(P. ciliaris)*, with two differences: the lip of the crested fringed orchid flower is about ¼ inch long and the spur is much shorter than the flower pedicel that supports it. *Cristata*, the species name, means "crested or tassel-like at the tips," referring to the fringed tips of the petals that extend from each side of the dorsal sepals.

*Platanthera cristata*
crested fringed orchid

The plant is stout and tall, sometimes as tall as 3 feet, with two to four leaves and several leaflike bracts. As many as eighty bright orange flowers may be packed tightly into a long, slender raceme at the top of the stem. *P. cristata* is pollinated by bumblebees (*Bombus* spp.) (Catling and Catling 1991).

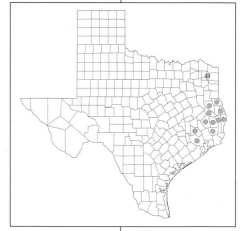

This orchid is considerably more rare than the yellow fringed orchid *(P. ciliaris)*. In the summer of 1987, we found a small population of crested fringed orchids blooming near a pond in Polk County, even though in the previous eight years, I found only water spider orchids *(Habenaria repens)* growing at that site. Roadside clearing in 1987 may have let in more light, allowing previously overlooked crested fringed orchid plants to bloom for the first time in several years. Its favored habitats are moist, sandy, intensely acid soils of baygalls, hillside seepage bogs, and wetland pine savannahs in the Pineywoods of East Texas.

Other Common Names: yellow fringed orchid, orange crest orchid, crested yellow orchid

TEXAS
DISTRIBUTION
Pineywoods

BLOOM TIME
June–July

GENERAL
DISTRIBUTION
Massachusetts south to Florida and west to Texas and Arkansas; throughout Deep South states

BLOOM TIME
June–September

## *Platanthera flava* var. *flava*

### SOUTHERN REIN ORCHID

The southern rein orchid bears ten to forty small flowers, each less than ½ inch wide. Although the species name *flava* means "pure yellow," the blooms actually appear to be yellow-green. The base of the lip has a fin-like knobby projection that partially obstructs the entrance to the nectar-containing spur. When an insect tries to reach this nectar, it is "reined" into contact with the sticky area that contains the pollinia. This probably explains the common name, "rein orchid," which, upon first hearing, many people believe to be "rain" orchid. Pollinators include mosquitoes, which are usually plentiful in the wet habitat of this orchid, and butterflies (Catling and Catling 1991).

The plant can grow to 2 feet tall, and has two or three dark green, slender oblong leaves that clasp the base of the stem. A small leaflike bract accompanies each flower.

The southern rein orchid is somewhat rare throughout its range, but it can be abundant in ideal habitats. With an ability to multiply from stoloniferous roots, it sometimes forms large colonies of hundreds of plants.

*Platanthera flava* var. *flava*
southern rein orchid

It often grows in standing water and prefers sites that are flooded each spring. It prefers the shade of densely forested floodplains and baygalls in the Pineywoods region of East Texas.

Frederick W. Thurow, a pioneer botanist who collected plants extensively in the Houston-Galveston area in the late nineteenth and early twentieth century, once recorded this species growing in Harris County (Correll 1944). In early June 1994, botanist Larry Brown discovered it again in southeast Harris County. At this site, several hundred plants, sometimes forming large colonies, are scattered along a low drainage channel in a prairie depression that is now wooded with large Chinese tallow trees *(Sapium sebiferum).* These populations of *Platanthera flava* var. *flava* may represent a fairly recent colonization from nearby populations. This shade-loving orchid is almost never recorded from sunny, open prairies and probably established itself here only after a non-native, invasive, and fast-growing tallow woodland formed.

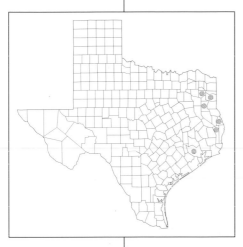

In the newly discovered Harris County site, *P. flava* var. *flava* was growing in black clay in the dappled shade of tallow trees. Plants associated with it here include southern wax myrtle *(Myrica cerifera),* swamp smartweed *(Polygonum hydropiperoides),* shiny coneflower *(Rudbeckia nitida),* lance-leaved water willow *(Justicia lanceolata),* lance-leaf Indian plantain *(Cacalia lanceolata),* eastern gama grass *(Tripsacum dactyloides),* spike-rush *(Eleocharis microcarpa),* and southern dewberry *(Rubus* spp.). The majority of southern rein orchids here appeared healthy, supporting robust spikes of flowers.

Other Common Names: tubercled orchid, pale green orchid

OPPOSITE PAGE
*Platanthera flava*
var. *flava*
southern rein orchid

TEXAS
DISTRIBUTION
Harrison, Jasper, Rusk, Sabine, and Upshur Counties in the Pineywoods; Harris County in the Gulf Prairies and Marshes

BLOOM TIME
June–July

GENERAL
DISTRIBUTION
Virginia to East Texas

BLOOM TIME
March–October

## Platanthera integra

GOLDEN
FROG
ARROW

The fringeless lip of the golden frog arrow distinguishes it from other fringe-tipped summer-blooming orange and yellow-orange *Platanthera*. The species name *integra,* Latin for "entire," refers to the unfringed lip.

The yellow-orange flowers, each about ½ inch long and densely packed into a slender raceme, are somewhat translucent and seem to glow in the bright August sun. When the lower flow-

*Platanthera integra*
golden frog arrow

## Lost and Found

In Texas, the golden frog arrow *(Platanthera integra)* is extremely rare. Until recently, the only known Texas documentation was a collection by Thomas Drummond in the 1800s, but we now know that this was based on a misidentification. Plant taxonomist W. C. Holmes (1983) discovered that the specimen had been misidentified when he was investigating the distribution and rarity of this orchid in Louisiana, Mississippi, and Texas. At the Gray Herbarium, he examined the Drummond specimen from Texas and determined that it was clearly *P. nivea,* not *P. integra.* With this finding by Holmes, it seemed likely that the golden frog arrow never grew in Texas. Some botanists believed that even if this orchid had ever occurred in Texas, it was probably extinct today.

In 1987, Steve Orzell, a botanist formerly with the Texas Parks and Wildlife Natural Heritage Program, and botanist Edwin Bridges located a herbarium specimen of *P. integra* collected from Texas. While examining specimens at the University of Texas Herbarium, a particular orchid attracted their attention. Mrs. J. L. Hooks had collected the plant on August 30, 1950, in Hardin County and correctly identified it as *Habenaria integra,* the former name for *P. integra.* However, an anonymous penciled notation on the specimen "corrected" her classification to *Habenaria nivea,* so the specimen was filed under the incorrect name. Orzell and Bridges affirmed that Mrs. Hooks's original identification was correct, which meant that *Platanthera integra* had been seen in Texas as late as the mid-twentieth century. This inspired Orzell and Bridges to search for the orchid in the wild. In August 1988 they found two populations growing in hillside seepage bogs in Jasper and Angelina Counties, conclusively dispelling the notion that the golden frog arrow was extinct in Texas (Bridges and Orzell 1989a).

ers begin to bloom, the inflorescence takes on a conical shape that later becomes a tight cylinder when the upper flowers open. The stem sometimes grows to 2 feet tall. It bears one or two long, slender clasping leaves and several leafy bracts.

This orchid prefers hillside seepage bogs and wetland pine savannahs. It ranges from North Carolina down the Atlantic seaboard to Florida, and along the Gulf Coast to Texas, with disjunct populations in the Pine Barrens of New Jersey and the mountains of North Carolina. This widely distributed orchid is rare throughout its range.

Other Common Names: yellow fringeless orchid, small southern yellow orchid

TEXAS DISTRIBUTION
Angelina, Hardin, and Jasper Counties in the Pineywoods

BLOOM TIME
July–September

GENERAL DISTRIBUTION
New Jersey to northern Florida and west to southeast Texas; North Carolina

BLOOM TIME
July–September

## *Platanthera lacera*

### RAGGED-FRINGED ORCHID

The green flower of the ragged-fringed orchid has a finely cut, greenish white, fringed lip that is alluded to in the species name *lacera,* which means "torn." The greenish white color of the lip, together with the fineness of the fringe, distinguishes it from all other members of the genus *Platanthera.* Twenty to forty green flowers may adorn the stout stem, which is clasped by slender, erect leaves. The plant grows from 10 to 30 inches tall. *P. lacera* is pollinated by sphinx moths (Catling and Catling 1991).

Donovan and Helen Correll discovered the ragged-fringed orchid in a moist woodland south of Dalby Springs in Bowie County, Texas, in June 1946 (Correll 1947). This discovery extended the range of this species about 200 miles southwest of Drew and Pope Counties in Arkansas, previously the farthest southwest this species was known to occur. Although considered common in the eastern United States, the ragged-fringed orchid is quite rare in Texas. This collection by the Corrells remains the only known record of this orchid in Texas. The Corrells say little about the habitat where the ragged-fringed orchid was found, mentioning only that it was in moist woods.

Except for a distinct preference for acidic soil, this orchid grows in a wide variety of habitats throughout much of eastern North America. Thriving in swamps, marshes, bogs, prairies, woodlands, and forests, the ragged-fringed orchid is rather indifferent to varying conditions of moisture, sunlight, and shade.

Other Common Names: green fringed orchid, ragged orchid

TEXAS
DISTRIBUTION
Bowie County in the Pineywoods

BLOOM TIME
May–July

GENERAL
DISTRIBUTION
Nova Scotia to Ontario; all states east of the Mississippi River except Florida; Minnesota, Missouri, Arkansas, Texas

BLOOM TIME
May–September

OPPOSITE PAGE
*Platanthera lacera*
ragged-fringed orchid
(photographed in
southern Arkansas)

## Platanthera nivea

### SNOWY ORCHID

The snowy orchid has from twenty to fifty vibrant white flowers, each less than ½ inch long. The species name *nivea* means "snow white," and except for the yellow-tinged column, the flowers are entirely white. In contrast to most orchids of the genus *Platanthera,* this one has a backward-curving lip that is dorsal in position. The spur is about ⅔ inch long, and is nearly horizontal except for the tip, which curves sharply upward. The

*Platanthera nivea*
snowy orchid

slender stem can reach up to 3 feet tall, with two or three lancelike leaves near its base.

It ranges from southern New Jersey down the Atlantic Coast to Florida and appears along the Gulf Coast as far west as Texas. It was once a common sight in the vast pine savannahs of the Big Thicket in East Texas, where large colonies of several hundred snowy orchids dominated parts of the landscape with white each June. It is now rare in Texas, since many of these wetlands were drained for development and pine plantations.

The snowy orchid occurs most frequently in the sunny wetland pine savannahs of Hardin, Jasper, Newton, and Tyler Counties. It often grows with a variety of colorful wildflowers. These include the ten-angle pipewort *(Eriocaulon decangulare)*, yellow-eyed grass (*Xyris* spp.), yellow savannah milkwort *(Polygala ramosa)*, yellow meadow beauty *(Rhexia lutea)*, and the pine-woods rose-gentian *(Sabatia gentianoides)*. It has been reported from the wet prairies of Harris, Jefferson, Galveston, and Waller Counties. Its only protected sites are in the Big Thicket National Preserve.

Other Common Names: southern small white orchid, bog torch, frog spear, white frog arrow, savannah orchid, white rein orchid

TEXAS
DISTRIBUTION
Hardin, Jasper, Newton, Sabine, and Tyler Counties in the Pineywoods; Chambers, Galveston, Harris, and Jefferson Counties in the Gulf Prairies and Marshes; Waller County in the Blackland Prairies

BLOOM TIME
June–July

GENERAL
DISTRIBUTION
New Jersey south along Atlantic Coast to Florida and west along the Gulf Coast to Texas

BLOOM TIME
May–September

## Pogonia

*Pogonia* is from the Greek word *pogon,* meaning "haired" or "bearded." The only member of this genus in Texas is *P. ophioglossoides,* the rose pogonia.

At one time the genus *Pogonia* contained orchids that are now classified in *Cleistes, Triphora,* and *Isotria.* Several orchids once in this genus still retain *Pogonia* in their common names, including the spreading pogonia *(Cleistes* spp.), nodding pogonia *(Triphora trianthophora),* and whorled pogonia *(Isotria verticillata).*

Now only two species are in this genus: *Pogonia ophioglossoides,* which is native to North America, and *P. japonica,* a native of China and Japan.

## *Pogonia ophioglossoides*

### Rose Pogonia

The rose pogonia has from one to three lovely rose pink to white flowers. Each bloom emerges just above a separate leaflike bract near the top of the stem. The flowers, which are about 1 inch wide, are composed of three elliptical sepals and two oblong petals. The spoon-shaped lip of the flower is veined with crimson-purple and is bearded with numerous yellow bristly projections (Catling and Catling 1991). The flower emerges just above a leaflike bract. A solitary leaf is positioned about halfway up the 8-inch to 14-inch stem. The roots of this orchid are slender and fibrous. *P. ophioglossoides* is pollinated by bees.

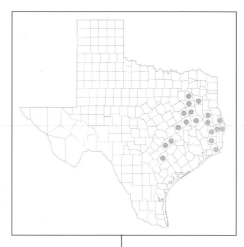

The rose pogonia grows in the acidic soils of wetland pine savannahs, in hillside seepage bogs, and on the edges of baygalls, mainly in the Pineywoods region. It also occurs in hillside seepage bogs in the Post Oak Savannah region of East Texas. In both regions, it requires a constant source of seepage water. Plants found nearby often include sphagnum moss, royal fern *(Osmundia regalis)*, and pitcher plant *(Sarracenia alata)*.

The rose pogonia is sometimes confused with the grass pink orchid *(Calopogon tuberosus)*, which often grows nearby, but the orchids bloom at different times. As the last flowers of the rose pogonia wither and fade, the blooms of the grass pink are just starting to open. The biggest difference between the species is structural: the lip of the rose pogonia is positioned at the lower

### The Scent of the Rose Pogonia: Sweet or Sour?

In his poem "Rose Pogonias," about finding a meadow with a thousand rose pogonias, Robert Frost described the air as "stifling sweet/With the breath of many flowers…." Mary Frances Baker, in *Florida Wild Flowers* (1926), said the rose pogonia "tantalizes with a suggestion of many perfumes." Other authors have likened its aroma to the sweet scent of raspberries (Gibson 1905).

In contrast, Thoreau wrote of this orchid (Summer 1884):"The adder's tongue arethusa *[Pogonia ophioglossoides]* smells exactly like a snake. How singular that in Nature, too, beauty and offensiveness should be thus combined. In flowers as well as persons we demand a beauty pure and fragrant which perfumes the air. The flower which is showy but has no odor, or an offensive one, expresses the character of too many mortals."

Fred Case (1987), an expert on Great Lakes orchids, called Thoreau's comparison of the orchid's odor to that of a snake "startling." Perhaps Thoreau, influenced by the orchid's common name, simply saw an opportunity to make a philosophical point. It is possible that Thoreau may have been influenced by Nathaniel Hawthorne's 1846 short story,"Rappaccini's Daughter," which illustrates a similar theme in the tale of a ravishingly beautiful young woman whose body is poisonous to touch.

*Pogonia
ophioglossoides* needs
a constant source of
seepage water.

part of the flower, in contrast to the uppermost lip of the grass pink orchid.

*Ophioglossoides,* the species name, derives from several Greek words that refer to a resemblance to a snake's tongue, and many of its common names refer to snakes. Despite this, most sources indicate that this orchid was named for its resemblance to the adder's tongue fern in the genus *Ophioglossum.*

Other Common Names: snake mouth orchid, adder's mouth, adder's tongue-leaved pogonia, beard flower, rose-crested orchid

TEXAS
DISTRIBUTION
Pineywoods and Post
Oak Savannah

BLOOM TIME
May–July

GENERAL
DISTRIBUTION
Newfoundland to
Ontario; Maine to
Florida and west to
Texas; Great Lakes
states; Kentucky,
Missouri, Arkansas

BLOOM TIME
March–August

OPPOSITE PAGE
*Pogonia
ophioglossoides*
rose pogonia

# Ponthieva

The genus *Ponthieva* is named for the French botanist Henri de Ponthieu, who collected plants in the Caribbean region and sent specimens to Sir Joseph Banks in England around 1778 (Correll 1950). This genus consists of approximately twenty-five species that are native to the warmer regions of North and South America. Although most of these species are terrestrial, a few are epiphytic. *P. racemosa,* the shadow witch, is the only member of this genus found in Texas.

## *Ponthieva racemosa*

### SHADOW WITCH

The elusive *Ponthieva racemosa* grows in the shade with ferns, liverworts, and mosses.

Shadow witch is a fitting name for this elusive orchid that grows in the shade of secluded haunts among ferns, liverworts, and mosses. It was unknown in Texas until Donovan and Helen Correll found it on July 18, 1946, along a muddy, tree-lined stream a few miles south of Jasper in Jasper County. Two days later, the Corrells found the shadow witch again at the "Devil's Slide near the town of Dayton in Liberty County." (That same summer, the Corrells found another orchid that had never before been recorded in Texas, the ragged-fringed orchid *[Platanthera lacera]* [Correll 1944].) Not seen again for many years, the shadow witch was rediscovered in Texas at a new location in Liberty County

in October 1993. At this location, it is found on the calcareous Dylan clay of the Flemming Formation. It grows near seepage springs on the banks of steep ravines along with southern shield fern *(Thelypteris kunthii)*.

The shadow witch is a showy orchid that sometimes grows 2 feet high. In autumn, a fuzzy reddish brown flower stalk with as many as thirty white flowers, each veined in green, emerges from a basal rosette of silky, green elliptical leaves. The concave pouchlike lip is uppermost and the two remaining petals form a landing pad for insect pollinators. Two winglike sepals, strongly marked in green, are positioned at the base of the lip, and the remaining sepal is concealed by the shieldlike petals.

It is usually found near limestone outcrops or in the calcareous soil of damp pine-hardwood forests, particularly on the rims and ledges of eroded stream banks and ravines.

Other Common Names: Ponthieu's orchid, glandular neottia

---

### Habitat or Heap: One Town's Choice

On July 20, 1946, two days after their discovery of the shadow witch in Texas, Donovan and Helen Correll found a second population of these plants. It was growing along a ravine bank known as the Devil's Slide on the east side of Dayton in Liberty County. This site is a complex of ravines, wooded with southern magnolias and pines, that cuts through the Trinity River bluff and exposes a calcareous, marly clay. Here, where the wet banks were once lavishly draped with southern shield fern *(Thelypteris kunthii),* the shadow witch once grew on the rims of eroded ledges.

Today this site is the Dayton city dump, meeting the fate of so many similar ravines, apparently considered by local residents as useless holes to be filled with garbage. Some of the ravines at the Dayton Devil's Slide still remain, and it is possible that the shadow witch grows nearby. We have searched for it there on many occasions, as have naturalists Geraldine Watson and Geyata Ajilvsgi. No one, however, has repeated the Corrells' discovery of the shadow witch at this once picturesque spot.

---

OPPOSITE PAGE
*Ponthieva racemosa*
shadow witch

---

TEXAS
DISTRIBUTION
Jasper and Liberty
Counties in the
Pineywoods

BLOOM TIME
September–October

GENERAL
DISTRIBUTION
Virginia south to Florida
and west to Texas

BLOOM TIME
February–October

## Schiedeella

The genus *Schiedeella* consists of six species native to the United States, Mexico, Guatemala, Honduras, Costa Rica, and the Greater Antilles (Garay 1980). In the United States, members of this genus have been recorded in Texas, New Mexico, and Arizona. The genus is named after Julius Wilhelm Schiede (1798–1836), a German botanist who collected many specimens in Mexico (Garay 1980). The only representative of this genus in Texas is the *S. parasitica,* red spot ladies tresses.

## *Schiedeella parasitica*

### Red Spot Ladies Tresses

As many as twelve widely spaced flowers, each about ⅓ inch long, are arranged in a very loose spiral on the red spot ladies tresses. The distinctive sharply down-turned lip of the flower flares outward, and is marked with three green lines with a depressed dark red spot in the center.

In original Greek usage, *parasitica* meant "one who eats at another's table at the other's expense." In bio-

*Schiedeella parasitica*
red spot ladies tresses

logical terms, a parasite derives nourishment from a host organism while providing nothing in return. At the time of its discovery, this orchid was thought to be parasitic because it was thought to lack both leaves and chlorophyll, so it was given the species name *parasitica*. In fact, this orchid does produce a basal rosette of deep green leaves after its blooms wither. Its slender, light brown stem, greenish on the lower portion, grows from 4 to 12 inches tall.

This orchid's tiny size and light coloration make it difficult to see among the litter of pine needles in the shade of montane conifer forests. It grows on shaded slopes along streams and canyons. *S. parasitica* was first collected in Texas from the Davis Mountains in Jeff Davis County by E. J. Palmer in 1926 (Correll 1944). This orchid was recently found again in the Davis Mountains at an elevation of 7,500 feet. It was fairly common on a north-facing slope in a montane conifer forest of ponderosa *(Pinus ponderosa)* and southwestern white pine *(P. stroboformis)*. Other prominent trees in the area include alligator juniper *(Juniperus deppeana),* gray oak *(Quercus grisea),* and gambel oak *(Q. gambelii)* (Bryant pers. com. 1997). This orchid also occurs above 7,000 feet in elevation in a forested canyon in the Guadalupe Mountains. It is rather common in the mountains of southern New Mexico, often growing near the striped coral root *(Corallorhiza striata)* and the spotted coral root *(C. maculata).*

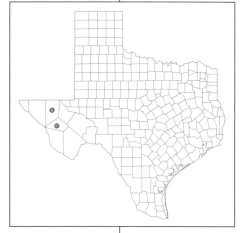

**TEXAS DISTRIBUTION**
Davis Mountains in Jeff Davis County, Guadalupe Mountains in Culberson County, Trans-Pecos Texas

**BLOOM TIME**
June–July

**GENERAL DISTRIBUTION**
Trans-Pecos Texas, New Mexico, and Arizona; Mexico

**BLOOM TIME**
June–September

# *Spiranthes*

The genus *Spiranthes* comprises forty-two species that grow primarily in temperate regions of North America and Eurasia. A few species are native to Central America and northern South America. Members of this genus are also found in Australia, New Caledonia, New Zealand, New Guinea, and Malaysia (Garay 1980). Thirteen species of *Spiranthes* are native to Texas. In fact, some of the most common orchids in the state are members of this genus. The spring-blooming *S. vernalis* and fall-blooming *S. cernua* are common roadside flowers in the entire eastern half of Texas. *Spiranthes* means "coiled flower," and the twisted or spiraling appearance of orchids in this genus is also reflected in common names such as ladies tresses and corkscrew orchids. Several species of *Spiranthes* are so similar in appearance that either a hand lens or a microscope is sometimes required to distinguish one from another. Identification of some species presents many problems to amateur and professional botanists. In members of this genus, many characteristics useful for taxonomic work that are present in living material are lost in dried herbarium specimens (Sheviak 1982).

## Spiranthes brevilabris

LADIES
TRESSES

In Latin, *brevilabris* means "short lip." The ladies tresses blooms in the spring and retains its three to five elliptical to lance-shaped yellow-green leaves beyond blooming time. This species has two varieties, *brevilabris* and *floridana*. Both occur in Texas.

## *Spiranthes brevilabris* var. *brevilabris*

### Texas Ladies Tresses

The Texas ladies tresses is characterized by its loose spiral of densely haired white to cream-colored flowers that are less than ¼ inch long. The lip is marked with yellow or sometimes with green, and has a dense tuft of hair on its margin. Three to five elliptical to lance-shaped leaves are present when the plant is in bloom. This orchid grows on sandy soil in moist prairies, pine-hardwood forests, and wetland pine savannahs in southeast Texas. The Texas ladies tresses orchid is rare throughout its range.

Other Common Names: None known

*Spiranthes brevilabris*
var. *brevilabris*
Texas ladies tresses

TEXAS
DISTRIBUTION
Galveston and Harris
Counties in the Gulf
Prairies and Marshes;
Cass and Tyler Counties
in the Pineywoods

BLOOM TIME
February–May

GENERAL
DISTRIBUTION
southern Georgia to
northern Florida, west
to Texas

BLOOM TIME
February–May

## Spiranthes brevilabris var. floridana

### FLORIDA LADIES TRESSES

The Florida ladies tresses differs from the Texas variety *(S. brevilabris* var. *brevilabris)* in that *S. brevilabris* var. *floridana* is hairless and its flowers scarcely spiral at all. The Florida variety also lacks the pronounced fringed margin on the lip. It grows in wet, sandy soil in wetland pine savannahs, pine-hardwood forests, and prairies of East Texas. This orchid, rare throughout its range, is represented by only five known herbarium collections from Texas.

Other Common Names: None known

### A Note on Taxonomy

As with so many matters of plant classification, some disagreement surrounds the two varieties of *Spiranthes brevilabris*. *S. brevilabris* was first described by John Lindley based on a specimen collected by Thomas Drummond in southeast Texas in the spring of 1840. Lindley described the flowers as being covered with short thick hairs and a finely fringed lip (Correll 1950).

A hairless variety of *S. brevilabris* was discovered in Florida in 1931 by Edgar T. Wherry, who named it *Ibidium floridana*. Donovan Correll (1950), however, considered both entities spring-blooming varieties of the late summer and fall-blooming *Spiranthes lacera* var. *gracilis*. Therefore, he named them *S. gracilis* var. *brevilabris* and *S. gracilis* var. *floridana*. Although both varieties resemble *S. gracilis,* they bloom in a different season, have a different distribution, and retain their leaves at bloom time. Because of these differences, Luer (1972) included both varieties in *S. brevilabris.*

TEXAS DISTRIBUTION
Harris County in the Gulf Prairies and Marshes; Hardin, Jefferson, and Tyler Counties in the Pineywoods

BLOOM TIME
February–May

GENERAL DISTRIBUTION
southern Georgia to northern Florida and west to Texas

BLOOM TIME
February–May

OPPOSITE PAGE
*Spiranthes brevilabris* var. *floridana*
Florida ladies tresses

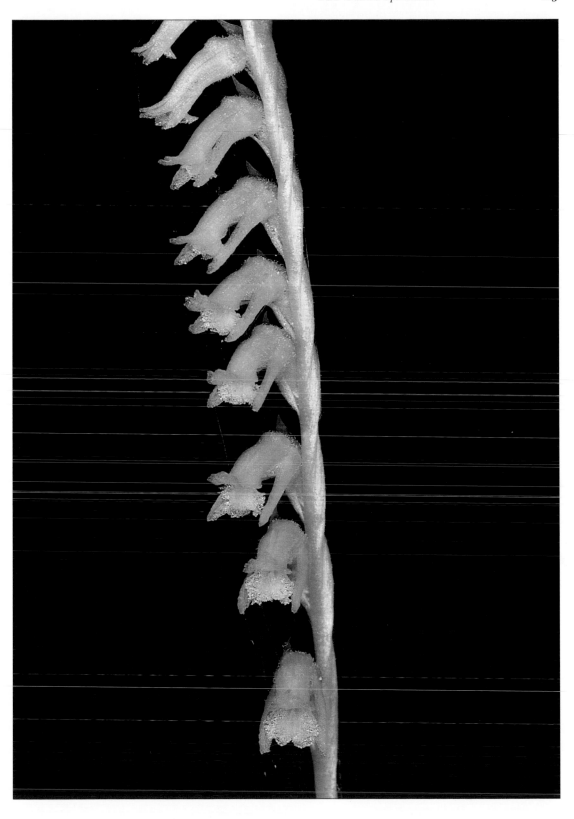

## *Spiranthes cernua*

### NODDING LADIES TRESSES

The nodding ladies tresses *(S. cernua)* is perhaps the most variable and wide-ranging ladies tresses in North America. It is a common sight in East Texas during October and November, sometimes flowering conspicuously in large numbers in open fields, roadsides, clearings, and even mowed lawns. It is also found in wetland pine savannahs, hillside seepage bogs, meadows, and clearings in pine-hardwood forests and upland woods. Once established, it often persists and blooms even in well-kept mowed lawns.

*Spiranthes cernua*
nodding ladies tresses

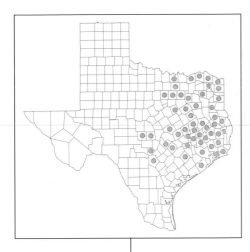

The stem bears as many as sixty pure white tubular flowers with inflated bases that form two to four spiral rows. The tubular corolla of the flower, about ¼ to ½ inch long, is formed from the downturned lip, the two lateral petals, and an overlapping dorsal sepal. The lateral sepals with curved-in tips are held closely parallel and almost touch the two lateral petals. The tips of the lip, the petals, and the dorsal sepal spread abruptly, giving the flower a gaping, open-mouthed appearance. The tendency of the flowers to droop slightly is recalled in the species name—*cernua*, Latin for "drooping"—and in the common name, the nodding ladies tresses. The lip, usually with a cream-colored center, is egg-shaped to oblong with a constricted middle and a broad base. In contrast to a closely related species, the flowers of *S. cernua* have little or no fragrance. The three to six fleshy lance-shaped leaves wither away before the flower appears. *S. cernua* is pollinated by bumblebees (*Bombus* spp.) (Catling and Catling 1991).

An abnormal form of *S. cernua* with closed flowers is also found in Texas, primarily in the Post Oak Savannah region. This closed-flowered condition resembles cleistogamy (auto-pollination with closed flowers), but here auto-pollination does not occur. In this closed-flowered form of *S. cernua*, seeds are produced by apomixis, a type of vegetative reproduction.

## *Spiranthes* Taxa

*Spiranthes* taxa are difficult for both plant taxonomists and amateur botanists to identify. The nodding ladies tresses, *S. cernua*, is perhaps the cause of much of this confusion. *S. cernua* is now recognized as a member of a species complex (the *S. cernua* complex) involving three other ladies tresses species: *S. ochroleuca* (yellow ladies tresses), *S. magnicamporum* (Great Plains ladies tresses), and *S. odorata* (fragrant ladies tresses) (Sheviak

1982). With genes acquired from hybridizing with other members of the complex, *S. cernua* displays a perplexing variety of forms. Even within a single population, the flowers of individual plants can vary greatly (Sheviak 1982). Three members of the *S. cernua* complex occur in Texas, *S. cernua, S. magnicamporum,* and *S. odorata. S. cernua* appears to be a hybrid resulting from crosses between other species in this complex and perhaps a pure ancestral form of *cernua* (Homoya 1993).

*S. cernua* can display an incredible variety of forms, often resembling other species in this complex and inhabiting a wide variety of habitats. At least three races of *S. cernua* are found in North America: one race reproduces sexually and forms seeds through pollination; one is sexually sterile but can produce seeds vegetatively through a process called apomixis; and one is an intermediate form, capable of producing seeds both vegetatively and sexually (Arditti 1992). Unlike *S. cernua, S. magnicamporum* and *S. odorata* have distinct habitat preferences. *S. magnicamporum,* a prairie species with intensely fragrant flowers, occurs only on calcareous soil in moist and dry grasslands. *S. odorata,* also with fragrant flowers, inhabits wet forested sites, primarily cypress-tupelo swamps that are often flooded in winter and spring. *S. cernua* is most frequent on moist to wet, acidic, sandy, or peaty soils, but occasionally occurs on calcareous soils. The flowers of *S. cernua* have little or no fragrance. Although it is often difficult to differentiate *S. magnicamporum* from *S. cernua,* it is easy to distinguish *S. odorata* because of its much larger flowers and its preference for swamps. *S. odorata* also retains its long, thick leaves when blooming, unlike *S. cernua* and *S. magnicamporum,* which shed their leaves before blooming. Interested readers are encouraged to read "Biosystematic Study of the *Spiranthes cernua* Complex" (Sheviak 1982) and "Morphological Variation in the Compilospecies *Spiranthes cernua*" (Sheviak 1991).

OPPOSITE PAGE
*Spiranthes cernua*
usually grows on
moist, acidic, sandy,
or peaty soils

*Spiranthes lacera* var. *gracilis*

SOUTHERN
SLENDER
LADIES
TRESSES

The small white flowers of the southern slender ladies tresses are about ¼ inch long, with a green-spotted lip. The species name *lacera,* Latin for "torn," describes the fringed margin of the lip. This orchid was formerly known in Texas as *S. gracilis;* however, Carlyle Luer (1975) recognized this orchid as a southern variety of *S. lacera.*

*Spiranthes lacera*
var. *gracilis*
Southern slender
ladies tresses

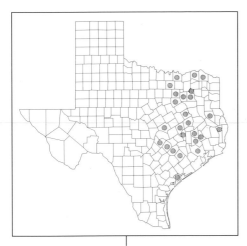

The variety name *gracilis*, a Latin word for "thin," alludes to the tall, slender shape of the plant. The stem is hairless, unlike some other *Spiranthes* orchids. A basal rosette of leaves forms early but is absent when the flowers appear.

This orchid, long-known as a "pioneer" plant, frequently grows in abandoned farmland, old fields, prairies, meadows, open woodlands, and roadsides. It is most common in the Post Oak Savannah region of east Central Texas.

Other Common Name: slender ladies tresses

TEXAS
DISTRIBUTION
Blackland Prairies,
Post Oak Savannah,
Pineywoods, Gulf
Prairies and Marshes,
Crosstimbers and
Prairies

BLOOM TIME
September–November

GENERAL
DISTRIBUTION
southern United States

BLOOM TIME
April–November

## Spiranthes laciniata

### Lace Lip Ladies Tresses

The lace lip ladies tresses often blooms profusely, with about fifty white to yellow flowers arranged in a single loose spiral on a stalk about 2 feet high. Robust plants grow to a height of about 4 feet. The species name *laciniata* means "jagged or unevenly cut," referring to the edge of the lip.

This orchid is easily confused with the earlier blooming spring ladies tresses *(S. vernalis);* however, the microscopic hairs on the flowers of *S. laciniata* are ball-tipped, but are pointed in *S. vernalis.* Another difference is that the projections on the base of the lip in *S. laciniata* are large and curve inward; in *S. vernalis,* they are short and cone-shaped.

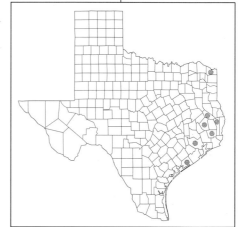

The lace lip ladies tresses is rare in Texas, in contrast to the very common spring ladies tresses. According to Donovan Correll (1944, 1950), the favored habitats of the lace lip ladies tresses are often flooded for part of each year, and include marshes, cypress swamps, ponds, and depressions in wetland pine savannahs and prairies in southeast Texas. It frequently grows in the company of lizard's tail *(Saururus cernuus),* arrowheads *(Sagitarria* spp.), saw grass *(Cladium jamaicense),* and spatter-docks *(Nymphaea* spp.). Carlyle Luer (1975) noted that it often grows on the banks of roadside ditches.

Donovan Correll (1950) once considered *S. laciniata* to be a hybrid of *S. vernalis* and *S. praecox,* but after further study, he treated it as a distinct species that is closely related to *S. praecox.*

Other Common Name: lace-lipped spiral orchid

TEXAS
DISTRIBUTION
Pineywoods and Gulf Prairies and Marshes

BLOOM TIME
May–July

GENERAL
DISTRIBUTION
New Jersey south to Florida and west to southeast Texas

BLOOM TIME
April–August

OPPOSITE PAGE
*Spiranthes laciniata*
lace lip ladies tresses

*Spiranthes longilabris*

GIANT
SPIRAL
ORCHID

The giant spiral orchid, with a barely spiraling spike of large flowers that bloom in late fall, is easily distinguished from other *Spiranthes* orchids. It is characterized by its long lip, alluded to in the species name *longilabris,* and by its bloom time, November and December. This late-flowering orchid should not be con-

*Spiranthes longilabris*
giant spiral orchid

fused with *S. vernalis* and *S. laciniata,* as these orchids bloom only in spring.

The plant can grow to a height of 20 inches, with a spike of as many as thirty flowers, each ½ inch long. Although Donovan Correll (1950) and Carlyle Luer (1975) both describe the lip as being white with a yellow center, Texas specimens appear to have a yellowish green lip.

This orchid is sparsely covered with tiny, club-shaped hairs. It has long been known to occur in Louisiana, where Thomas Drummond first collected it before 1840 (Correll 1950). In November 1945, it was collected for the first time in Texas by V. C. Cory near Kirbyville in Newton County (Correll 1947). In a remnant wetland pine savannah in Hardin County, *S. longilabris* grows in an open area with scattered, stunted pines *(Pinus palustris* and *P. taeda).* Associated plants at this sparsely vegetated, sandy site include rayless goldenrod *(Bigelowia nuttallii),* annual sundew *(Drosera annua),* Maryland milkwort *(Polygala mariana),* colic root *(Aletris aurea),* sweetbay magnolia *(Magnolia virginiana),* and southern wax myrtle *(Myrica cerifera).*

Today, it is known only from Hardin and Newton Counties, where it prefers wetland pine savannahs. Never common in Texas, it is becoming even more rare because of habitat loss.

Other Common Name: long lip ladies tresses

TEXAS DISTRIBUTION
Hardin and Newton Counties

BLOOM TIME
November–December

GENERAL DISTRIBUTION
Virginia south to Florida and west to Texas

BLOOM TIME
November–December

*Spiranthes magnicamporum*

GREAT PLAINS
LADIES
TRESSES

The Great Plains ladies tresses is adorned with many white to ivory-colored flowers, each about ½ inch long and spiraling around the stem in several ranks. This orchid has slender flowers with wide-spreading and ascending lateral sepals, and a yellow-centered ovate lip with a pronounced thickening in the center. The intensely fragrant flowers of *S. magnicamporum* exude the pleasant odor of coumarin, a substance used in perfumes and flavoring agents. Coumarin, with the characteristic odor of sweet clover (*Melilotus* spp.), is found in a variety of flowers.

*Magnicamporum,* the species name, is derived from Latin words meaning "great plains." Found primarily in the tallgrass prairie region of the Midwest, *Spiranthes magnicamporum* also appears in prairie remnants in disjunct populations in Ohio, Kentucky, Pennsylvania, Alabama, Georgia, Mississippi, Louisiana, and New Mexico.

*Spiranthes magnicamporum*
Great Plains ladies tresses

*Spiranthes magnicamporum* growing with seep muhly grass in Travis County

Somewhat rare in dense undisturbed grasslands, *S. magnicamporum* is more abundant in low, open prairies, especially where mild disturbances such as mowing and light grazing have removed competing vegetation. Soils where *S. magnicamporum* is found range from sands to clay loams, and are uniformly calcareous and slightly alkaline. In areas receiving plentiful rainfall in the eastern part of its range, it usually inhabits dry, well-drained, exposed sites on bluffs and sandy ridges. In the more arid western part of its range, it occupies relatively moist sites. At the western limits of its range, it is restricted to sites where it receives an almost continuous supply of seepage water (Sheviak 1982).

In Texas, the Great Plains ladies tresses ranges to the Edwards Plateau, the Crosstimbers and Prairies, the Blackland Prairies, and the Post Oak Savannah. It is usually found on open, moist slopes on limestone and calcareous rock outcrops and mowed banked roadsides. Although it can grow with non-native (introduced) grasses, it is frequently associated with a variety of native prairie grasses, including little bluestem *(Schizachyrium scoparium)*, seep muhly *(Muhlenburgia reverchonii),* Indiangrass *(Sorghas-trum nutans),* sideoats grama *(Bouteloua curtipendula),* hairy grama *(B. hiruta),* tall grama *(B. pectinata),* and silver bluestem *(Bothriochloa saccharoides).*

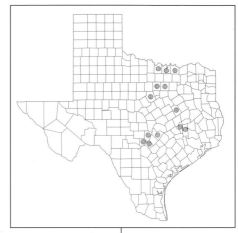

This orchid appears to be most abundant in Ashe juniper–oak series woodlands on the eastern edge of the Edwards Plateau. In this region, it often grows with seep muhly *(Muhlenburgia reverchonii)* and little bluestem *(Schizachyrium scoparium)* on rocky limestone slopes kept moist by seepage springs. When rain is plentiful, *Spiranthes magnicamporum* plants with robust spikes of large flowers may appear by the hundreds at such sites, but in dry years it may not flower at all.

*S. magnicamporum* is resistant to hard frosts, and blooms late in the year, sometimes in late January. Although some plants bloom earlier, flowering for the Great Plains ladies tresses peaks in late November. *S. magnicamporum* can easily be confused with the similar-looking *S. cernua* that usually grows in acidic soils. *S. magnicamporum* is distinguished by its preference for calcareous grassland habitat, its slender flowers with wide-spreading lateral sepals, a thickened fleshy lip, and a distinctive fragrance. The flowers of *S. cernua* are usually odorless or only faintly fragrant.

*S. magnicamporum* was first described as a new species by Charles J. Sheviak (1973). It was once considered a variety of *S. cernua,* but is now recognized as both a separate species and a member of the *S. cernua* complex. (Refer to the discussion under *S. cernua*). It is likely that some herbarium specimens from Texas that are identified as *S. cernua* may actually be *S. magnicamporum.* However, many of the characteristics that distinguish *S. magnicamporum* from *S. cernua* in living plants are lost in the preparation of herbarium specimens, making definitive determination of species extremely difficult (Sheviak 1982).

Other Common Name: prairie ladies tresses

TEXAS DISTRIBUTION
Edwards Plateau, Crosstimbers and Prairies, Blackland Prairies, Post Oak Savannah

BLOOM TIME
November–January

GENERAL DISTRIBUTION
Minnesota, North Dakota, and Michigan south to South Dakota, Nebraska, Iowa, Illinois, Indiana, Kansas, Missouri, Arkansas, Oklahoma, and Texas; disjunct populations in Ohio, Kentucky, Pennsylvania, Alabama, Georgia, Mississippi, Louisiana, and New Mexico

BLOOM TIME
September–January

## *Spiranthes odorata*

### Fragrant Ladies Tresses

In October, these tall, graceful orchids brighten the otherwise gloomy swamps. Their sweet fragrance—alluded to in the species name *odorata*—suggests a mixture of vanilla and jasmine. The large, creamy white blooms may spiral in several ranks. The yellow-centered lip is about ½ inch long, and tapers to a point.

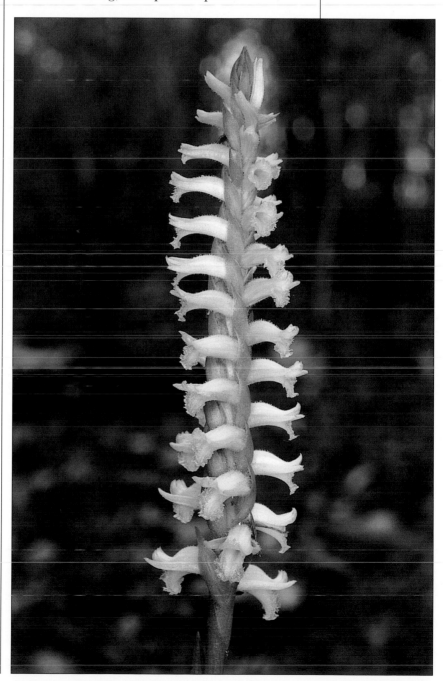

*Spiranthes odorata*
fragrant ladies tresses

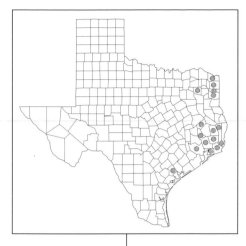

## The Vanilla Orchid

The aroma of the fragrant ladies tresses reminds many people of the scent of vanilla. In fact, vanilla is obtained from a tropical orchid, the climbing, vinelike *Vanilla planifolia,* which has large, yellow flowers. Flavoring is extracted from its cured, unripened capsules, which are like beans or pods. Madagascar is one of the largest producers of what is sometimes referred to as "the orchid of commerce."

Three to six leaves, each about 1 inch wide and nearly 15 inches long, extend upward from the base of the stem. Unlike most fall-blooming *Spiranthes* orchids, the leaves of *S. odorata* persist until after the flowers bloom. The plant can reach a height of about 3 feet. *S. odorata* is pollinatd by bumble-bees (*Bombus* spp.) (Catling and Catling 1991).

The fragrant ladies tresses often grows on muddy terraces and in standing water in baldcypress-tupelo swamps and floodplain forests in East Texas. In such environments, it frequently forms large colonies that reproduce from stoloniferous rhizomes. *S. odorata* is commonly associated with savannah panicum *(Panicum gymnocarpon)* and lizard's tail *(Saururus cernuus).*

Other Common Name: swamp tresses

TEXAS
DISTRIBUTION
Primarily in the Pineywoods; also reported from the Blackland Prairies, the Post Oak Savannah, and the Gulf Prairies and Marshes

BLOOM TIME
October–November

GENERAL
DISTRIBUTION
Virginia south to Florida and west along the Gulf Coast to Texas

BLOOM TIME
October–March

OPPOSITE PAGE
The tall, graceful *Spiranthes odorata* can grow three feet tall.

## Spiranthes ovalis

### OVAL LADIES TRESSES

Except for its small flowers, the rare oval ladies tresses resembles *S. cernua*, nodding ladies tresses. *Ovalis*, the species name, probably refers to the shape of the crowded inflorescence, which tapers at both ends.

The small white flowers, each less than ¼ inch long, spiral in multiple ranks on a disproportionately tall, slender stem growing up to 16 inches tall. Stems typically bear two to three lancelike, sheath-

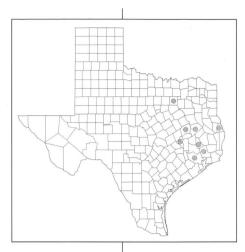

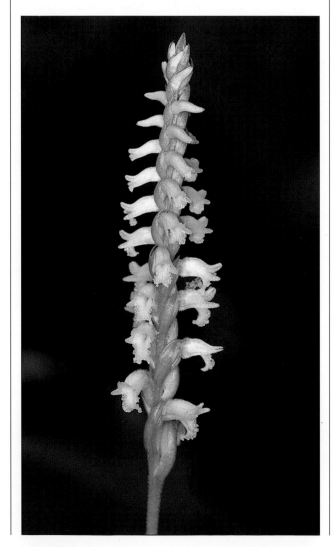

*Spiranthes ovalis.* oval ladies tresses

ing basal leaves and a few leafy bracts higher up. Unlike other fall-blooming ladies tresses that lose their leaves before blooming, the leaves of the oval ladies tresses persist until after the flowers bloom.

The oval ladies tresses grows only in the Blackland Prairies, the Post Oak Savannah, and the Pineywoods of East Texas. It inhabits moist, humus-rich soil along streams in floodplain forests, baldcypress-tupelo swamps, pine-hardwood forests, and oak woodlands. Unlike most members of the *Spiranthes* genus, the oval ladies tresses is quite tolerant of shade and can bloom under a fairly dense forest canopy (Case 1987). Although *S. ovalis* ranges throughout much of North America, it is a rare plant, occurring only infrequently.

Other Common Names: lesser ladies tresses, little elephants

## John Lindley: Father of Orchid Classification (1799–1865)

The oval ladies tresses was first described and named by Dr. John Lindley, an English botanist who pioneered modern orchidology. He based his 1840 description on a specimen collected by Thomas Drummond somewhere in East Texas (Correll 1950). Years earlier, in 1825, Lindley had begun his trailblazing work in the classification of the orchid family, a project that consumed him until his death forty years later. For thirty-one of those years (1829–1860), he also served as Chair of Botany at University College in London. Lindley's many publications include *Folia Orchidaceae* (1852–1859) and *An Introduction to the Natural System of Botany* (1830); in the latter, he espoused a "natural" system of plant classification. His methods of classifying orchids have been revised over time, but the basics of his system remain intact. In his honor, the American Orchid Society calls their scientific journal *Lindleyana*.

TEXAS
DISTRIBUTION
Blackland Prairies,
Post Oak Savannah,
Pineywoods

BLOOM TIME
September–November

GENERAL
DISTRIBUTION
Virginia west to
Missouri and south to
Florida, west to Texas
and Oklahoma

BLOOM TIME
September–November

*Spiranthes parksii*

NAVASOTA
LADIES
TRESSES

The Navasota ladies tresses is the most famous of all Texas orchids, perhaps because it is the only orchid in the state officially listed as an endangered species. The cream-colored flowers grow in a loose spiral covering about 2 inches of the stalk, which reaches a height of 8 to 15 inches. The short, rounded petals with a green stripe in the center, the oval lip, and the green bracts

*Spiranthes parksii*
Navasota ladies tresses

## The Orchid That Stopped a Highway

The Navasota ladies tresses *(Spiranthes parksii)* was first discovered along the Navasota River in October 1945 by H. B. Parks. Parks believed it to be an unusual representative of *S. lacera* var. *gracilis*. Later, Donovan Correll (1947) examined the specimen and declared it to be a new species, naming it in honor of its finder. For more than thirty years, the Navasota ladies tresses eluded researchers, including Correll, Carlyle Luer, and Marshall Johnston. H. B. Parks remained the only person to have seen it in the wild. Because decades had passed since it had been recorded, the Smithsonian Institution declared it extinct in 1975.

A researcher visiting the Oakes Ames Herbarium at Harvard University in that same year, 1975, discovered a clue that might mean the Navasota ladies tresses was not extinct after all. Paul Catling, a botanist from the University of Toronto, noticed that several specimens of *Spiranthes* orchids collected by Parks, who was by then deceased, were from a site 10 miles west of the original Navasota ladies tresses discovery. Although they were labeled *S. cernua*, a common species, he was sure that some of them were actually *S. parksii*. Even though many botanists had been looking for *S. parksii*, apparently Catling was the first interested party to notice these particular specimens (Catling and McIntosh 1979).

Inspired by this find, Catling headed to Texas with K. L. McIntosh to search the second location in hopes of finding the elusive orchid. On October 25, 1978, they explored a post oak woodland northwest of the town of Navasota. They knew it was not a good year for *Spiranthes* orchids, because local residents reported that there had been little rain that summer. Even *S. cernua* and *S. lacera* were not as commonly found as in other years.

Catling and McIntosh explored the banks of an eroded gully surrounded by post oaks, blackjack oaks, and American beautyberry shrubs, and found several *Spiranthes* orchids growing in an open grassy area. Some of the flowers were closed forms of *S. cernua*, but others had open, greenish white flowers with short, rounded petals; an oval, abruptly ending lip; and a bract with a distinctive white tip. A close examination revealed that these orchids were definitely the long lost Navasota ladies tresses. Catling and McIntosh found seven orchids at that spot, and a few hundred yards away, on the banks of another eroded gully, thirteen more plants (Catling and McIntosh 1979).

The saga of the Navasota ladies tresses does not end there, however. The sites found that day in 1978 by Catling and McIntosh were the only known locations for Navasota ladies tresses, when in May 1982, the U.S. Fish and Wildlife Service gave the orchid official protection under the Endangered Species Act. The following year, something else was planned for the Navasota area: widening and expansion of State Highway 6. These plans were abruptly put on hold in July 1983, when the U.S. Fish and Wildlife Service declared that the proposed expansion of State Highway 6 would jeopardize the survival of the Navasota ladies tresses. However, the fragile habitat of the orchid did not stay protected for long. In September U.S. Fish and Wildlife reversed their jeopardy statement, citing a new survey showing additional populations of the Navasota ladies tresses elsewhere, and the highway expansion was allowed to proceed. But since most of the newly discovered populations are on private land, survival of this species is not necessarily guaranteed.

with white tips distinguish this species from other *Spiranthes* orchids.

This endemic Texas orchid is found primarily in the Post Oak Savannah region of East Texas. It grows in small gravelly openings on the banks of eroded gullies in post oak woodlands along with black jack oak, yaupon, American beautyberry, and little bluestem grass (Poole and Riskind 1987, Orzell 1990). In October 1986, the Navasota ladies tresses *(S. parksii)* was found in Angelina National Forest in Jasper County (Bridges and Orzell 1989a, Orzell 1990). Before this discovery in the

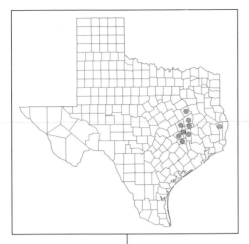

Pineywoods region, *S. parksii* was thought to be confined to the Post Oak Savannah region of east Central Texas. At this woodland site in Angelina National Forest, more than 100 miles east of the Post Oak Savannah region, *S. parksii* occurs as scattered individual plants in shallow, nutrient-poor soil that is associated with the Catahoula Sandstone Barrens. Not surprisingly, this woodland community in Angelina National Forest is quite similar to the woodland sites where *S. parksii* grows in the Post Oak Savannah region. In Angelina, it grows on the upper ends of small creeks in an open woodland of stunted post oak *(Quercus stellata)* and Texas black hickory *(Carya texana)*. Understory shrubs in this woodland include farkleberry *(Vaccinium arboreum)* and yaupon *(Ilex vomitoria)*.

**OPPOSITE PAGE**
An endangered species in Texas, **Spiranthes parksii** grows in gravelly soil in eroded gullies in post oak woodlands.

TEXAS

DISTRIBUTION

Brazos, Burleson, Freestone, Grimes, Lee, Madison, Robertson, and Washington Counties in the Post Oak Savannah; Jasper County in the Pineywoods

BLOOM TIME
October–November

GENERAL

DISTRIBUTION

Texas only

## Spiranthes praecox

### GIANT LADIES TRESSES

The spring-blooming giant ladies tresses prospers on roadsides and in fields, pine-hardwood forests, wetland pine savannahs, prairies, and open woodlands in East Texas. Only the spring ladies tresses *(S. vernalis),* which blooms about the same time, is more common.

The giant ladies tresses sometimes grows as high as 30 inches. As many as forty white flowers, each about ½ inch long, grow in a spiral pat-tern that varies greatly from plant to plant. Texas specimens are of-ten tightly spiraled in several ranks. The plant typically has five or six lancelike, linear leaves about ½ inch wide and 10 inches long. The diverging green lines on the lip distinguish *S. praecox* from all other *Spiranthes* orchids.

Roadside mowing, suspended during the spring wildflower sea-son, allows this orchid to flourish. The species name, *praecox,* is Latin for "very early," alluding to its early bloom time.

Other Common Names: grass-leaved ladies tresses, grass-leaf ladies tresses

TEXAS
DISTRIBUTION
Pineywoods, Post Oak
Savannah, Blackland
Prairies, Gulf Prairies
and Marshes

BLOOM TIME
April–May

GENERAL
DISTRIBUTION
Rhode Island to Florida
and west to Texas and
Arkansas

BLOOM TIME
February–September

OPPOSITE PAGE
*Spiranthes praecox*
giant ladies tresses

**Spiranthes tuberosa**

LITTLE
LADIES
TRESSES

The little ladies tresses, with flowers less than ⅕ inch long, has the tiniest flowers of all *Spiranthes* orchids in North America. Although it may reach a height of 2 feet and bear as many as thirty flowers, it is difficult to spot from a distance, and may be more common than is realized. The tiny, pure white flowers are arranged on the flimsy, slender stem in a single spiral, sometimes tightly coiled; at other times, so loosely coiled it could scarcely be called a spiral.

*Spiranthes tuberosa*
little ladies tresses

A basal rosette of three small, somewhat egg-shaped leaves with pointed ends emerges in late summer and lasts through the winter and into spring. The leaves then wither and disappear by late spring, just before the orchid flowers bloom in early summer. This tiny orchid is quite similar in form to *S. lacera* var. *gracilis*. However, *S. lacera* var. *gracilis* has a striking green blotched lip, is considerably larger in size, and blooms in the fall.

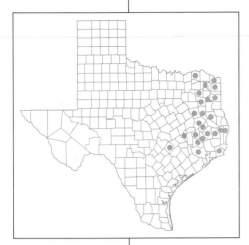

The species name, *tuberosa*, is from Latin words meaning "swollen" or "tuberous," alluding to a tuberlike root produced by the plant every year. Sometimes the tuber on an older plant lasts for two years. The tuberous root is a distinctive feature of this species of *Spiranthes*.

The little ladies tresses occurs mainly in the Pineywoods and the Post Oak Savannah regions of East Texas. It prefers open, sandy pine-hardwood forests and oak woodlands, especially well-drained sites that are often quite dry by summer.

Other Common Names: little pearl twist, Beck's ladies tresses

TEXAS DISTRIBUTION
Pineywoods, Post Oak Savannah, Blackland Prairies, Gulf Prairies and Marshes

BLOOM TIME
June–September

GENERAL DISTRIBUTION
Massachusetts south to central Florida, west to Texas, and north to Arkansas, Missouri, Kentucky, and Illinois; throughout the Deep South states

BLOOM TIME
June–October

## Spiranthes vernalis

### SPRING LADIES TRESSES

**TEXAS DISTRIBUTION**
Pineywoods, Gulf Prairies and Marshes, Post Oak Savannah, Blackland Prairies, Rolling Plains

**BLOOM TIME**
April–July

**GENERAL DISTRIBUTION**
Vermont and New Hampshire south to Florida and west to Texas; Virginia west to Kansas and north to Nebraska; throughout Deep South states

**BLOOM TIME**
February–August

The spring ladies tresses is undoubtedly the most common orchid in Texas. The species name, *vernalis,* means "spring," the time when this orchid sometimes lines the roadsides for miles. When roadside mowing is suspended on major highways in Texas each spring, the spring ladies tresses reaches its full glory, blooming profusely. When mowing resumes later in the season, the orchid benefits again, because mowing helps control competing vegetation.

The white flowers, which may number as many as fifty, are densely covered with fine, pointed hairs, a feature that distinguishes this from other *Spiranthes* orchids. The lip is about ⅓ inch long and is marked with a yellow center. Flowers usually spiral in a single rank that is tightly coiled up the stem.

An older plant sometimes reaches a height of 3½ feet, but even a 6-inch-tall plant can bloom. The average height is around 20 inches.

*S. vernalis* can tolerate a wide variety of habitats, including roadsides, pastures, prairies, oak woodlands, pine-hardwood forests, wetland pine savannahs, floodplain forests, marshes, and even beaches and offshore islands. Tolerant of saline soil, it can grow in brackish marshes.

The spring ladies tresses was first described in 1845 by George Engelmann and Asa Gray, based on a specimen collected on Galveston Island, Texas, by the German botanist Ferdinand J. Lindheimer (Correll 1950).

Other Common Names: upland ladies tresses, spring tresses

*If spring came but once a century instead of once a year, or burst forth with the sound of an earthquake . . . what wonder and expectation there would be in all hearts to behold the miraculous change.*

HENRY WADSWORTH LONGFELLOW

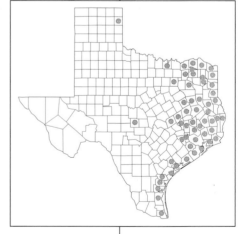

**OPPOSITE PAGE**
*Spiranthes vernalis*
spring ladies tresses

## Stenorrhynchos

The genus *Stenorrhynchos* consists of nine orchid species (Garay 1980) with large and showy flowers. Most are found in Central and South America, but one, *S. michuacanus* (Michoacan ladies tresses) ranges as far north as Trans-Pecos Texas and Arizona. The genus name comes from the Latin *stenos,* meaning "narrow," and *rhynchos,* meaning "snout," in reference to the slender rostellum of the flowers in this genus.

## *Stenorrhynchos michuacanus*

MICHOACAN
LADIES
TRESSES

This orchid is named after Michoacán, the state in Mexico where it was first collected in 1825. Although it is common in Mexico, it is very rare in the United States, growing only in a few sites in Texas and Arizona.

The Michoacan ladies tresses usually grows from 8 to 16 inches tall, although it can sometimes reach a height of about 30 inches. A stout stem supports an elongated spike of twenty-five to thirty

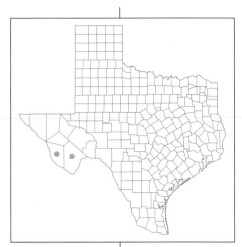

*Stenorrhynchos michuacanus*
Michoacan
ladies tresses

tubular-shaped, densely hairy flowers that are about ¾ inch long, white to yellow-green, and striped with blue-green.

Three to five slender leaves form a rosette at the base of the plant, but then wither away before the flowers bloom. Even the sheathing bracts on the flower stem dry up and turn brown before the flowers open.

The Michoacan ladies tresses grows on rocky slopes along intermittent streams of canyons in the brushy, oak-juniper-pinyon pine woodlands of the Chisos Mountains in Brewster County.

In 1880, Valery Havard collected the first specimen from the United States from the Chinati Mountains in Presidio County, Texas. The following year, Mr. and Mrs. John Gill Lemmon collected it in the Chiricahua Mountains of Cochise County, Arizona. However, after these initial discoveries in the United States, it remained unrecorded for sixty-four years (Correll 1950). Recognized by Donovan Correll (1944), the unidentified Havard specimen at the United States National Herbarium was included in his "Flora of Texas" *(Orchidaceae)*. A few years ago, the orchid was reported growing at high elevations in the Chisos Mountains.

Other Common Names: None known

TEXAS DISTRIBUTION
Brewster and Presidio Counties in Trans-Pecos Texas

BLOOM TIME
October

GENERAL DISTRIBUTION
Texas, Arizona; Mexico

BLOOM TIME
September–February

## Miles to the Michoacan

The late October morning was cool as I ascended a steep trail into the high Chisos Mountains in Big Bend National Park, looking for one of the rarest orchids in Texas. After five miles of hiking, including a 2,000-foot climb, I arrived at the head of a rocky stream bed and followed a twisting route along a brushy, boulder-strewn canyon. I noticed a tributary to the left, so I turned and followed it for a while. I soon decided I was not going in the direction indicated by my crude map, hastily scrawled during a telephone conversation with someone who had seen the orchid years before. Instead of reversing my steps, I decided to climb a ridge and hike down into another canyon which I believed to be the correct one. Realizing that I was still lost, I climbed up the canyon wall for a better view. Recognizing the familiar face of Emory Peak and orienting myself, I resumed my quest.

Somewhat discouraged now, I walked another half mile and suddenly, there it was: the rare Michoacan ladies tresses, green stripes and all, growing on a grassy, dry, rocky slope above a stream bed, together with bear grass, lechuguilla, juniper, oak, and pinyon pine. As my frustration turned to joy, I set up my photographic equipment and took the picture you see in this book.
(Joe Liggio, 1999)

## Tipularia

The genus *Tipularia* is named for the cranefly *Tipula illustris* because of the shape of the flowers. *Tipularia* comprises only three geographically isolated species: *T. josephi,* which grows in the Himalayan Mountains; *T. japonica,* which grows in Japan; and *T. discolor,* which grows in the United States. At one time, members of this genus were probably more widely distributed in Asia and North America than they are today.

## *Tipularia discolor*

### CRANEFLY ORCHID

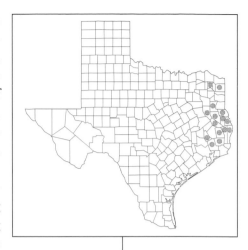

If one asymmetrical flower of the cranefly orchid can be said to resemble a cranefly, a full stalk with as many as forty blooms conceivably resembles an entire swarm of craneflies. The widely spaced, drooping flowers, each about ½ inch across, are translucent and greenish, mottled with purple. The petals are arranged asymmetrically, with one overlapping the dorsal sepal. A 1-inch-long spur protrudes from the base of the three-lobed lip, and the lobe in the middle of the lip is elongated. *T. discolor* is pollinated by medium-sized moths (Catling and Catling 1991).

*Tipularia discolor*
cranefly orchid

Solitary green leaves of *Tipularia discolor* emerge in the fall and lie flat on fallen leaves until spring.

In late autumn, when the hardwoods in the forest canopy are bare and the ground is littered with fallen leaves, a solitary green leaf emerges from the orchid's tuberous root. This broad, fleshy leaf, dark green on top and a rich purple on the underside, lies flat against the fallen leaves on the forest floor, exposed to the bright winter sun. *Discolor,* the species name, probably alludes to the different colors in the leaf.

During the winter, the plant photosynthesizes starches and stores them in its tuberous roots. In spring, shade from the newly leaved forest canopy causes the solitary leaf to wither away, and the plant remains dormant for several months while the rest of the forest comes to life.

By late summer the leafless stalk, inconspicuous in the deep shade because of its tiny flowers, emerges and may grow to a height of about 2 feet. Even if many plants have produced a single leaf months before, only a few of them will bloom now. When the flowers fade, the stalk remains until the seed capsules ripen.

The cranefly orchid inhabits rich, moist, pine-hardwood forests, growing on slopes and beside streams. It often grows in the company of beech trees.

Other Common Name: elfin spur

TEXAS DISTRIBUTION
Pineywoods

BLOOM TIME
August–September

GENERAL DISTRIBUTION
Massachusetts west to Nebraska, along the Atlantic Coast to north Florida, west to Texas and Arkansas; abundant in the Appalachian states

BLOOM TIME
July–September

# Triphora

The genus *Triphora* comprises twelve species of terrestrial orchids that grow only in the Western Hemisphere. Most of these orchids are small with slender stems; several small, clasping leaves; and fleshy, tuberous roots. They prefer shaded forest floors, and often grow in leaf mold or on rotting logs.

*Triphora,* the genus name, combines two Greek words that mean "three-fold" and "bearing," probably a reference to the fact that the plant often bears three flowers at a time.

## *Triphora*
## *trianthophora*

### Three
### Birds
### Orchid

The species name, *trianthophora*, combines three Greek words: *tri* ("three"), *antho* ("flower"), and *phora* ("bearing"). Indeed, this orchid usually bears three flowers at once. They develop in sequence, with one in bud, one in bloom, and one fading from bloom.

The common name, three birds orchid, refers to the three flowers and their superficial resemblance to birds. Despite the name, this orchid occasionally has as many as six flowers. Each flower is white tinged with pink, with a three-lobed lip about ½ inch long and two petals that form a hood over the lip and three spreading sepals. The fleshy, maroon-tinged stem grows 2 to 10 inches tall, and is clasped by two to eight heart-shaped leaves.

*Triphora
trianthophora*
three birds orchid

*It is a secret of the world that all things subsist and do not die, but only retire a little from sight and afterwards return again. Nothing is dead . . . .*

Ralph Waldo Emerson

*T. trianthophora* is pollinated by small bees, mostly *Augochlora pura* (Catling and Catling 1991).

The three birds orchid seems to be rare in East Texas, but it may be more common than is realized. Its small size and inconspicuous appearance, particularly when not in bloom, and its sporadic emergence, make it difficult to locate. It prefers moist, sandy soil rich in leaf litter near streams in pine-hardwood and floodplain forests.

Other Common Name: nodding pogonia

**Surprise Appearance**

One of the most rewarding moments in orchid hunting can be the morning you find a flock of three birds orchids all blooming at the same time. Arriving on such a morning may involve looking for the plants for several years, and then—when you find some of the plants—returning every few days to observe their progress.

The reason for this is that the three birds orchid is well known for being common in a particular location one year and almost impossible to find the next. This curious situation is brought about by the orchid's ability to remain underground for a long time while the tuberous roots live saprophytically, that is, on decaying matter, with the aid of a mycorrhizal fungus. Under favorable conditions, plants generate many stoloniferous buds, allowing rapid multiplication at a given site. This can result in a riot of blooming orchids. Under less favorable conditions, few or no plants at all may emerge.

If the plant sprouts at all, it does so in midsummer and develops buds in one or two weeks, although it may be several more weeks before they open for pollination. Then, all mature buds within a colony of plants bloom on the same day. This simultaneous flowering enhances the chances of cross-pollination, and appears to be triggered by a drop in temperature, often associated with thunderstorms or rainy weather. If the temperature drops a few degrees, the orchids bloom *en masse* 48 hours later, typically opening before noon and lasting only one day. A second set of blooms may appear about three weeks later.

TEXAS DISTRIBUTION
Pineywoods

BLOOM TIME
July–September

GENERAL DISTRIBUTION
All states east of the Mississippi River; Iowa, Nebraska, Kansas, Missouri, Oklahoma, Arkansas, Louisiana, Texas

BLOOM TIME
July–November

# Zeuxine

The genus *Zeuxine* is a small group of terrestrial orchids native to Africa and Asia, with one species, *Zeuxine strateumatica,* now naturalized in Texas. *Zeuxine,* the genus name, is derived from a Greek word meaning "joining," referring to the partial union of the lip and the column.

## *Zeuxine strateumatica*

ZEUXINE
ORCHID

The Zeuxine orchid, a relative newcomer to Texas, can be covered with up to fifty white flowers, each with a bright yellow lip about ⅙ inch long. It grows to 10 inches tall, and has from five to twelve sword-shaped leaves that sheathe the stem.

In the southern United States, it thrives in mowed lawns, under shrubs, and even in gardens and outdoor flowerpots. This perennial orchid seems to behave like an annual weed and usually appears in different places from year to year. With creeping rhizomes, it can produce new plants at new locations from lateral branching buds (Sheehan and Sheehan 1995).

Other Common Names: None known

### A "Naturalized Citizen" of the Wild Orchid Community

*Zeuxine strateumatica* was first discovered in Indian River County, Florida, in 1936. In a few short years, it was widespread throughout Florida, growing on roadsides and lawns and cropping up most unexpectedly in gardens, flowerpots, and even through the cracks in sidewalks.

In 1938, orchidologist Oakes Ames published a fascinating account of how this orchid from a distant part of the world became so widespread in Florida (Correll 1950). He speculated that the seeds of *Z. strateumatica* had "stowed away" in large shipments of centipede grass *(Eremochloa ophiuroides)* imported from China to Florida and other southern states. Because centipede grass was sold widely in Georgia, Florida, and Gulf Coast states as far west as Louisiana, Ames predicted that the orchid would soon be commonplace in those states.

In 1989, *Z. strateumatica* was discovered for the first time in Texas, growing in a mulched flower bed in Montgomery County: a 10,000-mile journey from China. It has since been recorded from Harris County as well.

TEXAS
DISTRIBUTION
Harris and Montgomery
Counties in the Gulf
Prairies and Marshes,
Pineywoods

GENERAL
DISTRIBUTION
Georgia, throughout
Florida, Gulf Coast states
west to Texas

BLOOM TIME
December–January

OPPOSITE PAGE
*Zeuxine
strateumatica*
Zeuxine orchid

*Appendix A*

# SOURCES OF

# SCIENTIFIC NAMES

The scientific names used in this book closely follow *Vascular Plants of Texas: A Comprehensive Checklist including Synonymy, Bibliography, and Index* (Jones et al. 1997). However, we have adopted a different name for the yellow Lady's slipper collected in Bailey County. According to Sheviak (1995), the name for this orchid should be *Cypripedium parviflorum* var. *pubescens* (Willdenow) Knight.

*Calopogon*
    *C. oklahomensis* D. H. Goldman
    *C. tuberosus* (L.) Britton, E. Sterns, &
        J. Pottenburg var. *tuberosus*
*Cleistes*
    *C. bifaria* (M. Fernald) P. M. Catling &
        K. B. Gregg
*Corallorhiza*
    *C. maculata* (C. Rafinesque-Schmaltz)
    *C. odontorhiza* (C. Von Willdenow) T. Nuttall
    *C. striata* J. Lindley
    *C. wisteriana* S. Conrad
*Cypripedium*
    *C. kentuckiense* C. F. Reed
    *C. parviflorum* var. *pubescens* (C. Von Willdenow)
        J. Knight
*Deiregyne*
    *D. confusa* L. Garay
*Dichromanthus*
    *D. cinnabarinus* (P. de la Llave & J. de Lexarza)
        L. Garay
*Epipactis*
    *E. gigantea* D. Douglas ex. W. Hooker
*Habenaria*
    *H. quinqueseta* (A. Michaux) A. Eaton
        var. *quinqueseta*
    *H. repens* T. Nuttall

*Hexalectris*
    *H. grandiflora* (A. Richard & H. Galeotti)
        L. O. Williams
    *H. nitida* L. O. Williams
    *H. revoluta* D. Correll
    *H. spicata* (T. Walter) Barnhart var. *spicata*
    *H. spicata* var. *arizonica* (S. Watson)
        P. M. Catling & V. S. Engel
    *H. warnockii* O. Ames & D. Correll
*Isotria*
    *I. verticillata* (G. H. Muhlenberg ex. C. Von
        Willdenow) C. Rafinesque-Schmaltz
*Listera*
    *L. australis* J. Lindley
*Malaxis*
    *M. macrostachya* (J. de Lexarza) K. E. O. Kuntze
    *M. unifolia* A. Michaux
    *M. wendtii* G. Salazar
*Platanthera*
    *P. blephariglottis* (C. Von Willdenow) J. Lindley
        var. *conspicua* (G. Nash) C. Luer
    *P. chapmanii* (J. K. Small) C. Luer emend. Folsom
    *P. ciliaris* (C. Linnaeus) J. Lindley
    *P. clavellata* (A. Michaux) C. Luer
    *P. cristata* (A. Michaux) J. Lindley
    *P. flava* (C. Linnaeus) J. Lindley var. *flava*
    *P. integra* (T. Nuttall) A. Gray ex. L. Beck
    *P. lacera* (A. Michaux) G. Don var. *lacera*
    *P. nivea* (T. Nuttall) C. Luer
*Pogonia*
    *P. ophioglossoides* (C. Linnaeus) A. L. de Jussieu
*Ponthieva*
    *P. racemosa* (T. Walter) C. Mohr
*Schiedeella*
    *S. parasitica* (A. Richard & H. Galeotti)
        F. Schlechter

*Spiranthes*
    *S. brevilabris* var. *brevilabris* J. Lindley
       var. *brevilabris*
    *S. brevilabris* J. Lindley var. *floridana*
       (E. Wherry) C. Luer
    *S. cernua* (C. Linnaeus) L. C. Richard
    *S. lacera* (C. Rafinesque-Schmaltz) var. *gracilis*
       (J. Bigelow) C. Luer
    *S. laciniata* (J. K. Small) O. Ames
    *S. longilabris* J. Lindley
    *S. magnicamporum* C. Sheviak
    *S. odorata* (T. Nuttall) J. Lindley
    *S. ovalis* J. Lindley var. *ovalis*

    *S. parksii* D. Correll
    *S. praecox* (T. Walter) S. Watson
    *S. tuberosa* C. Rafinesque-Schmaltz
    *S. vernalis* G. Engelman & A. Gray
*Stenorrhynchos*
    *S. michuacanus* (P. de la Llave & J. de Lexarza)
*Tipularia*
    *T. discolor* (F. Pursh) T. Nuttall
*Triphora*
    *T. trianthophora* (O. Swartz) P. Rydberg
*Zeuxine*
    *Z. strateumatica* (C. Linnaeus) F. Schlechter

*Appendix B*

# EXCLUDED SPECIES

Several orchid species have been reported by some writers as being native to Texas, but most scientists do not consider these orchids to be Texas species. Such species are referred to as "excluded species." These species are discussed in this appendix.

*Calopogon barbatus* (Walter) Ames
    *C. barbatus* does not grow in Texas. All plants and herbarium material previously referred to as *C. barbatus* from Texas are now recognized as *C. oklahomensis* (Goldman 1995).
*Epidendrum conopseum* R. Brown in Aiton
    Donovan Correll did not find this epiphytic orchid in Texas, but wrote that it was likely to be found in swamp-forests of southeastern Texas, since he had found it nearby in Lake Charles, Louisiana, in Calcasieu Parish (Correll 1944). The Louisiana site is only 30 miles from the Texas border.
*Erythrodes querceticola* (Lindley) Ames
    Oakes Ames was the first writer to include Texas in the range of *Erythrodes querceticola*, "low erythrodes." He reported one herbarium record from Texas (in *An Enumeration of the Orchids of the United States and Canada,* 1924). Donovan Correll did not see any herbarium specimens of this species from Texas, but wrote that it was likely to be found in swamps and hardwood forests in Texas, since it was known to be abundant in nearby West Feliciana Parish, Louisiana ("Flora of Texas," *Orchidaceae,* 1944). If it grows in Texas, this inconspicuous orchid will probably be found in the swamps, moist hardwood forests, and wooded ravines of East Texas. Since no specimen has been found in Texas, Marshall C. Johnston excluded it from his list (*The Vascular Plants of Texas,* 1990).

*Platanthera limosa* Lindley
    Donovan Correll (1944) reports that this species was collected in the valley of the Rio Grande below Dona Ana, New Mexico, by C. C. Perry, J. M. Bigelow, and Charles Wright on the Mexican Boundary Survey in 1849. Correll stated that this orchid should be expected to occur in Texas, since this area is less than 50 miles from the Texas border. However, no one has yet found it in Texas.
*Spiranthes romanzoffiana* A. von Chamisso
    Marshall C. Johnston included *S. romanzoffiana* in his Texas list (*Vascular Plants of Texas,* 1990) based on a specimen at the University of Michigan Herbarium recorded as having been collected near Amarillo, Texas. However, according to Anthony A. Reznicek (pers. com. 1991), Curator of the University of Michigan Herbarium, the record is almost certainly in error. The identification of the species was correct, but the recorded location is in question. The specimen was included in a poorly documented collection donated to the University of Michigan by Oldenburg College.

    In the late nineteenth century, monks from Oldenburg College made several collecting trips to Colorado, New Mexico, and the Texas Panhandle. One packet collected by Father Diamede contained numerous specimens from the Texas Panhandle, and the specimen identified as *S. romanzoffiana* was included in that packet. This species inhabits the most northerly ranges of the *Spiranthes* genus, occurring as far north as the Arctic Circle, and is not at all likely to grow in the hot Texas Panhandle. Father Diamede's specimen was probably collected at a high elevation in New Mexico or Colorado, where this species is known to grow at elevations of at least 9,000 feet.

*Appendix C*

# Species Distribution by County

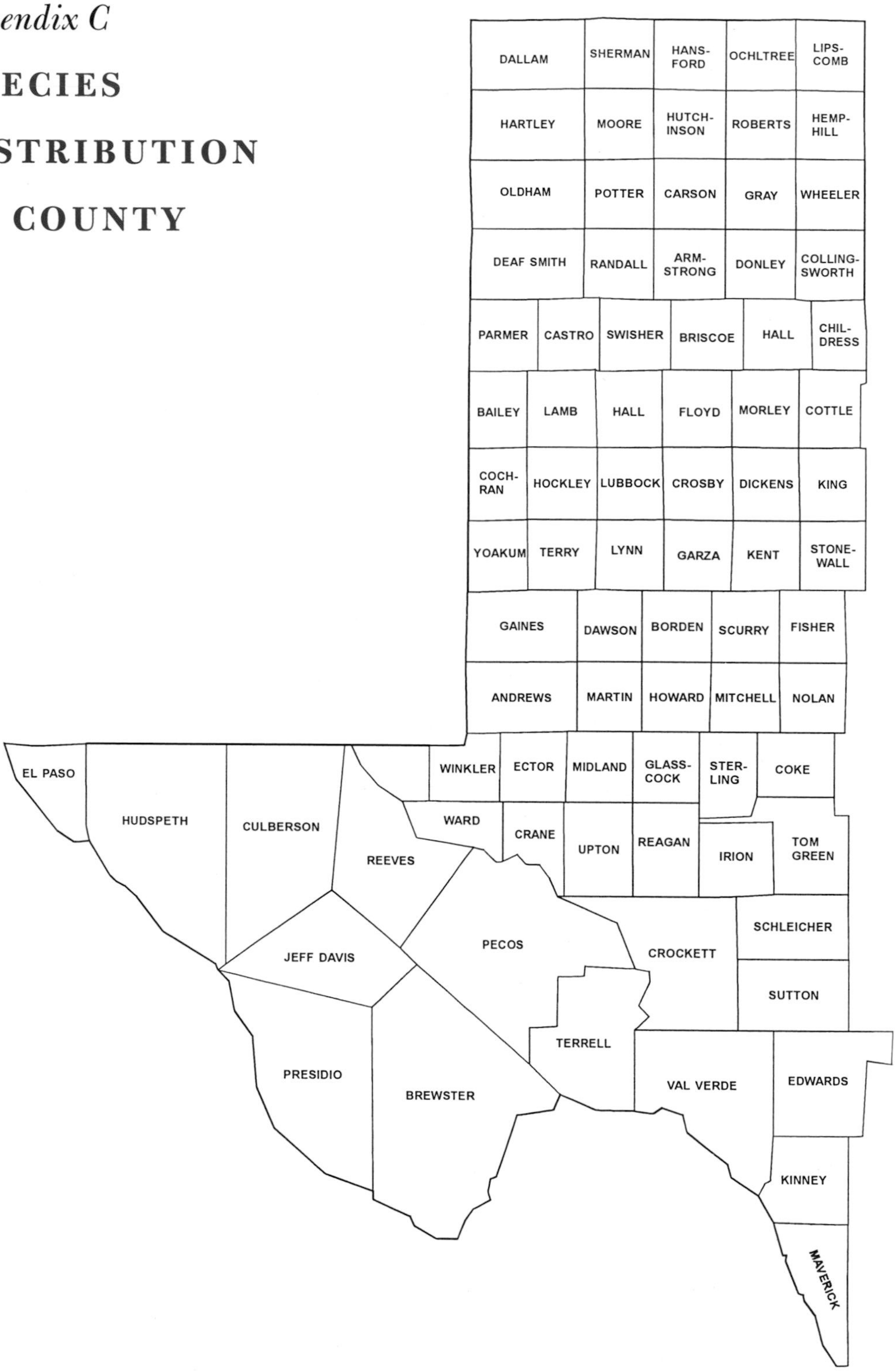

| | |
|---|---|
| *Calopogon oklahomensis* | Brazos, Hardin, Harris, Henderson, Lamar, Leon, Nacogdoches, Polk, San Augustine, Titus, Tyler |
| *Calopogon tuberosus* | Anderson, Angelina, Chambers, Freestone, Hardin, Houston, Jasper, Jefferson, Leon, Newton, Robertson, Sabine, Smith, Tyler, Walker |
| *Corallorhiza maculata* | Brewster, Jeff Davis |
| *Corallorhiza odontorhiza* | Cass, Red River |
| *Corallorhiza striata* | Culberson, Presidio |
| *Corallorhiza wisteriana* | Anderson, Bandera, Bexar, Blanco, Bowie, Brazoria, Brazos, Chambers, Cherokee, Dallas, Fannin, Freestone, Goliad, Gregg, Hardin, Harris, Harrison, Hays, Henderson, Houston, Jasper, Jefferson, Lamar, Liberty, Limestone, Kerr, Marion, McLennan, Medina, Morris, Nacogdoches, Newton, Red River, Sabine, San Augustine, San Jacinto, Tom Green, Travis, Tyler |
| *Cypripedium kentuckiense* | Cass, Harrison, Nacogdoches, Newton, Red River, Sabine, San Augustine, Shelby, Tyler |
| *Cypripedium parviflorum* var. *pubescens* | Bailey |
| *Deiregyne confusa* | Brewster |
| *Dichromanthus cinnabarinus* | Brewster |
| *Epipactis gigantea* | Austin, Bandera, Blanco, Brewster, Culberson, Dallas, Edwards, Garza, Gillespie, Gonzales, Hays, Kendall, Kerr, Presidio, Real, San Saba, Sutton, Travis, Uvalde, Val Verde, Wise |
| *Habenaria repens* | Anderson, Bastrop, Brazos, Cameron, Anderson, Bastrop, Brazos, Cameron, Cass, Fort Bend, Freestone, Gonzales, Guadalupe, Hardin, Houston, Jasper, Milam, Montgomery, Nacogdoches, Polk, Tyler, Van Zandt, Walker, Wood |
| *Hexalectris grandiflora* | Brewster, Jeff Davis |
| *Hexalectris nitida* | Bandera, Bell, Bexar, Blanco, Bosque, Brewster, Comal, Coryell, Dallas, Hays, Kendall, Kerr, Pecos, Somervell, Taylor, Travis, Uvalde |

| | |
|---|---|
| *Hexalectris revoluta* | Brewster, Culberson |
| *Hexalectris spicata* var. *arizonica* | Anderson, Brewster, Culberson, Dallas, Palo Pinto, Travis |
| *Hexalectris spicata* var. *spicata* | Austin, Bexar, Brazos, Brewster, Brown, Calhoun, Cass, Cherokee, Coke, Dallas, Hardin, Harris, Houston, Jackson, Jeff Davis, Kendall, Presidio, Tarrant, Tom Green, Travis, Tyler, Victoria |
| *Hexalectris warnockii* | Brewster, Dallas, Gillespie, Hays, Jeff Davis, Presidio, Real, Taylor, Terrell |
| *Isotria verticillata* | Cass, Jasper, Nacogdoches, Newton, Polk, Sabine, San Augustine, Tyler |
| *Listera australis* | Angelina, Bowie, Cass, Cherokee, Hardin, Harris, Jasper, Jefferson, Liberty, Marion, Montgomery, Nacogdoches, Newton, Sabine, San Augustine, San Jacinto, Shelby, Smith, Titus, Tyler |
| *Malaxis macrostachya* | Jeff Davis, Presidio |
| *Malaxis unifolia* | Angelina, Cherokee, Harris, Houston, Jasper, Morris, Nacogdoches, Newton, Red River, San Augustine, Tyler |
| *Malaxis wendtii* | Brewster |
| *Platanthera blephariglottis* var. *conspicua* | Galveston |
| *Platanthera chapmanii* | Hardin, Jefferson, Orange, Tyler |
| *Platanthera ciliaris* | Angelina, Bowie, Cass, Henderson, Houston, Jasper, Milam, Montgomery, Nacogdoches, Newton, Polk, Sabine, San Jacinto, Smith, Titus, Tyler, Wood |
| *Platanthera clavellata* | Anderson, Angelina, Bowie, Cass, Cherokee, Harrison, Jasper, Liberty, Montgomery, Morris, Nacogdoches, Newton, Sabine, San Jacinto, Titus, Tyler |
| *Platanthera cristata* | Angelina, Hardin, Harris, Jasper, Montgomery, Morris, Nacogdoches, Newton, Polk, Sabine, Shelby, Tyler |
| *Platanthera flava* var. *flava* | Harris, Harrison, Jasper, Rusk, Sabine, Upshur |

| | |
|---|---|
| *Platanthera integra* | Angelina, Hardin, Jasper |
| *Platanthera lacera* | Bowie |
| *Platanthera nivea* | Chambers, Galveston, Hardin, Harris, Jasper, Jefferson, Newton, Sabine, Tyler, Waller |
| *Pogonia ophioglossoides* | Anderson, Angelina, Bastrop, Freestone, Gonzales, Hardin, Henderson, Houston, Jasper, Jefferson, Lee, Leon, Nacogdoches, Newton, Robertson, Sabine, Smith, Tyler, Van Zandt |
| *Ponthieva racemosa* | Jasper, Liberty |
| *Schiedeella parasitica* | Culberson, Jeff Davis |
| *Spiranthes brevilabris* var. *brevilabris* | Cass, Galveston, Harris, Tyler |
| *Spiranthes brevilabris* var. *floridana* | Hardin, Harris, Jefferson, Tyler |
| *Spiranthes cernua* | Angelina, Bastrop, Bell, Bexar, Bowie, Brazoria, Brazos, Cass, Chambers, Colorado, Cooke, Dallas, Denton, Fannin, Freestone, Grimes, Hardin, Harris, Harrison, Henderson, Hill, Houston, Lamar, Leon, Liberty, Llano, Jasper, Jefferson, Kaufman, Kendall, Madison, Mason, Milam, Montgomery, Nacogdoches, Navarro, Parker, Polk, Red River, Robertson, Rusk, San Augustine, Tarrant, Titus, Travis, Trinity, Tyler, Walker, Washington, Wood |
| *Spiranthes lacera* var. *gracilis* | Bastrop, Bell, Brazos, Calhoun, Chambers, Colorado, Dallas, Denton, Ellis, Fayette, Freestone, Grayson, Harris, Jasper, Kaufman, Lamar, Leon, Montgomery, Nacogdoches, Raines, Red River, Robertson, San Jacinto, Travis, Van Zandt, Walker |
| *Spiranthes laciniata* | Angelina, Bowie, Hardin, Harris, Jasper, Matagorda, Polk |
| *Spiranthes longilabris* | Hardin, Newton |
| *Spiranthes magnicamporum* | Blanco, Brazos, Comal, Cooke, Erath, Grayson, Grimes, Kendall, Limestone, Montague, Parker, Tarrant, Travis |
| *Spiranthes odorata* | Bowie, Cass, Chambers, Hardin, Harris, Harrison, Jasper, Jefferson, Liberty, Marion, Orange, San Jacinto, Trinity, Tyler, Victoria |

| | |
|---|---|
| *Spiranthes ovalis* | Brazos, Dallas, Harris, Houston, Leon, Liberty, Sabine, San Jacinto |
| *Spiranthes parksii* | Brazos, Burleson, Freestone, Grimes, Jasper, Leon, Madison, Robertson, Washington |
| *Spiranthes praecox* | Angelina, Brazos, Cass, Chambers, Galveston, Hardin, Harris, Harrison, Jasper, Jefferson, Liberty, Madison, Morris, Nacogdoches, Newton, Orange, Polk, Sabine, San Augustine, San Jacinto, Shelby, Trinity, Tyler, Walker, Waller, Wood |
| *Spiranthes tuberosa* | Anderson, Bastrop, Bowie, Brazos, Cass, Cherokee, Gregg, Harris, Harrison, Houston, Jasper, Jefferson, Lamar, Montgomery, Nacogdoches, Newton, Polk, San Jacinto, Smith, Titus, Trinity, Tyler, Walker, Wood |
| *Spiranthes vernalis* | Anderson, Angelina, Aransas, Austin, Bowie, Brazoria, Brazos, Calhoun, Cameron, Camp, Cass, Chambers, Cherokee, Cooke, Dallas, Delta, Fannin, Fort Bend, Freestone, Galveston, Grimes, Hardin, Harris, Harrison, Hemphill, Hopkins, Houston, Hunt, Jasper, Jefferson, Kenedy, Kleberg, Lamar, Leon, Liberty, Mason, Matagorda, Montgomery, Milam, Nacogdoches, Newton, Nueces, Panola, Polk, Red River, Robertson, San Jacinto, San Patricio, Shelby, Tyler, Upshur, Van Zandt, Victoria, Walker, Waller |
| *Stenorrhynchos michuacanus* | Brewster, Presidio |
| *Tipularia discolor* | Angelina, Cass, Cherokee, Hardin, Jasper, Liberty, Nacogdoches, Newton, Polk, Rusk, Sabine, San Augustine, San Jacinto, Shelby, Titus, Tyler |
| *Triphora trianthophora* | Anderson, Jefferson, Nacogdoches, San Jacinto, Smith |
| *Zeuxine strateumatica* | Harris, Montgomery |

Specimens examined for county orchid distribution were found in the following Texas herbariums:

- Angelo State University (ASTC)
- Stephen F. Austin University (AS)
- Baylor University (BAYLU)
- Botanical Research Institute of Texas (BRIT)
- Lamar State University (Lamar)
- Spring Branch Science Center (SBSC)
- Sul Ross State University (SRSC)
- Texas A&M University (TAES & TAMU)
- University of Texas (TEX)
- University of Texas at El Paso (UTEP)
- Texas Tech University (TTC)
- Southwest Texas Junior College (UVST)

Additional distribution records for other species were obtained from:

- Correll (1944, 1947) for several species
- Catling and Engel (1993) for *Hexalectris spicata* var. *arizonica*
- Goldman (pers. com. 1995) for *Calopogon oklahomensis*

# Literature Cited

Ajilvsgi, Geyata. 1979. *Wildflowers of the Big Thicket: East Texas and Western Louisiana.* College Station: Texas A&M University Press.

Amerson, Peggy A., Austin Lodwick, Laurence N. Lodwick, and David H. Riskind. 1975. The incredible orchid family. *Texas Parks & Wildlife* (October) 16–20.

Ames, Oakes. 1924. *An enumeration of the orchids of the United States and Canada.* Boston: The American Orchid Society.

Amos, Bonnie B., and Frederick R. Gehlbach, eds. 1988. *Edwards Plateau vegetation.* Waco, Tex.: Baylor University Press.

Arditti, Joseph. 1992. *Fundamentals of orchid biology.* New York: John Wiley.

Atwood, J. T. 1985. The range of *Cypripedium kentuckiense. American Orchid Society Bulletin* 54: 1197–1199.

Bridges, Edwin L., and Steve L. Orzell. 1989a. Additions and noteworthy vascular plant collections from Texas and Louisiana, with historical, ecological and geographical notes. *Phytologia* 66 (1): 12–69.

————. 1989b. Longleaf pine communities of the west Gulf coastal plain. *Natural Areas Journal* 9 (4): 246–263.

Case, Frederick W., Jr. 1987. *Orchids of the western Great Lakes region.* 2d ed. Saginaw, Mich.: Cranbrook Institute of Science.

Catling, P. M., and K. L. McIntosh. 1979. Rediscovery of *Spiranthes parksii* Correll. *Sida* 8: 188–193.

Catling, Paul M., and Katharine B. Gregg. 1992. Systematics of the genus *Cleistes* in North America. *Lindleyana* 7 (2): 57–73.

Catling, Paul M., and Victor S. Engel. 1993. Systematics and distribution of *Hexalectris spicata* var. *arizonica* (Orchidaceae). *Lindleyana* 8 (3): 119–125.

Catling, Paul M., and Vivian R. Catling. 1991. A synopsis of breeding systems and pollination in North American orchids. *Lindleyana* 6 (4): 187–210.

Correll, Donovan S. 1947. Additions to the orchids of Texas. *Wrightia* 1 (3): 166–182.

————. 1938. *Cypripedium calceolus* var. *pubescens.* Harvard University Botanical Museum Leaflets 7: 1–18.

————. 1950. *Native orchids of North America.* Waltham, Mass.: Chronica Botanica Company.

————. 1944. *Orchidaceae.* Vol. 3, pt. 3, Flora of Texas. Renner, Tex.: Texas Research Foundation.

Correll, Donovan S., and Marshall C. Johnston. 1979. *Manual of vascular flora of Texas.* Richardson: University of Texas at Dallas.

Darwin, Charles. 1890. *The various contrivances by which orchids are fertilised by insects.* 2d ed. London: John Murry.

Diamond, D. D., D. H. Riskind, and S. L. Orzell. 1987. A framework for plant community classification and conservation in Texas. *Texas Journal of Science* 39: 203–221.

Doherty, John W. 1997. The genus *Cypripedium.* Pt. II, Mycorrhizal fungus. *North American Native Orchid Journal* 3 (1): 45–58.

Dressler, Robert L. 1981. *The Orchids: Natural History and Classification.* Cambridge, Mass., and London: Harvard University Press.

Engel, Victor. 1987. Saprophytic orchids of Dallas. *American Orchid Society Bulletin* 56 (8): 831–835.

Folsom, James P. A. 1984. Reinterpretation of the status and relationships of the yellow-fringed orchid complex. *Orquidea* (Mexico) 9 (2): 337–345.

Freudenstein, John V. 1997. A monograph of *Corallorhiza* (Orchidaceae). *Harvard Papers in Botany* 10: 5–51.

Garay, L. A. 1980. A generic revision of the *Spiranthinae.* Harvard University Botanical Museum Leaflets 28 (4): 277–426.

Gehlbach, Frederick R. 1988. Forests and woodlands of the northeastern Balcones Escarpment. In *Edwards Plateau vegetation,* edited by Bonnie B. Amos and Frederick R. Gehlbach, 57–77. Waco, Tex.: Baylor University Press.

Geiser, S. W. 1948. *Naturalists of the frontier.* 2d ed. Dallas, Tex.: Dallas University Press.

Goldman, Douglas H. 1995. A new species of *Calopogon* from the midwestern United States. *Lindleyana* 10 (1): 37–42.

Gould, F. W., G. O. Hoffman, and C. A. Rechenthin. 1960. Vegetational areas of Texas. Agricultural Extension Service L-492.

Gunter, A. Y. 1972. *The Big Thicket.* Austin, Tex.: Jenkins Publishing Co.

Harley, J. L., and S. E. Smith. 1983. *Mycorrhizal symbiosis.* London: Academic Press.

Hatch, Stephan L., Kancheepuram N. Gandhi, and Larry E. Brown. 1990. *Checklist of the vascular plants of Texas.* Mp-1655. College Station: Texas Agricultural Experiment Station.

Holmes, W. C. 1983. The distribution of *Habenaria integra* (Nutt.) Spreng. (Orchidaceae) in Mississippi, Louisiana, and Texas. *The Southwestern Naturalist* 28 (4): 451–456.

Homoya, Michael A. 1993. *Orchids of Indiana.* Bloomington and Indianapolis: Indiana University Press, Indiana Academy of Science.

Johnston, Marshall C. 1990. 2d ed. *The vascular plants of Texas: A list, updating the manual of the vascular plants of Texas.* Austin, Tex.: Marshall C. Johnston. Self-published.

Jones, Stanley D., Joseph K. Wipff, and Paul Montgomery. 1997. *Vascular plants of Texas: A comprehensive checklist including synonymy, bibliography, and index.* Austin: University of Texas Press.

Koopowitz, Howard, and Hilary Kaye. 1983. Plant extinction: A global crisis. Washington, D.C.: Stone Wall Press.

Luer, Carlyle A. 1972. *The native orchids of Florida.* Bronx: New York Botanical Garden.

———. 1975. *The native orchids of the United States and Canada.* Bronx: New York Botanical Garden.

MacRoberts, B. R., and M. H. MacRoberts. 1997. Floristics of beech-hardwood forests in East Texas. *Phytologia* 82 (1): 20–29.

MacRoberts, M. H., and B. R. MacRoberts. 1995. Noteworthy vascular plant collections on the Kisachie National Forest, Louisiana. *Phytologia* 78 (4): 291–313.

Magrath, Lawrence K. 1939. Nomenclatural notes on *Calopogon, Corallorhiza,* and *Cypripedium* (Orchidaceae) in the Great Plains region. *Sida* 13 (3): 371.

Marks, P. H., and P. A. Harcombe. 1975. Community diversity of coastal plain forests in southeast Texas. *Ecology* 56: 1004–1008.

———. 1981. Forest vegetation of the Big Thicket, southeast Texas. *Ecological Monogram* 51: 287–303.

Nixon, E. S. 1985. *Trees, shrubs, and woody vines of East Texas.* Nacogdoches, Tex.: Bruce Lyndon Cunningham Productions.

Nixon, E. S., and J. R. Ward. 1986. Floristic composition and management of East Texas pitcher plant bogs. In *Wilderness and natural areas in the eastern United States: A management challenge,* edited by D. L. Kulhavy and R. N. Conner, 283–287. Nacogdoches, Tex.: Stephen F. Austin State University.

Nixon, E. S., B. L. Ehrahart, S. A. Jasper, J. S. Neck, and J. R. Ward. 1983. Woody, streamside vegetation of Prairie Creek in East Texas. *The Texas Journal of Science* 35: 205–213.

Orzell, Steve L. 1990. *Inventory of national forests and national grasslands in Texas.* Austin: Texas Natural Heritage Program.

Orzell, Steve L., and Edwin L. Bridges. 1987. Further additions and noteworthy collections in the flora of Arkansas, with historical, ecological, and phytogeographic notes. *Phytologia* 64 (2): 81–144.

Ospina, H. Mariano. 1996. Orchidology and biotechnology. *Orchids, the Magazine of the American Orchid Society,* 1072–1074.

Pijl, L. Van Der, and C. H. Dodson. 1966. *Orchid flowers, their pollination and evolution.* Coral Gables, Fla.: University of Miami Press.

Poole, Jackie M., and David H. Riskind. 1987. *Endangered, threatened, or protected native plants of Texas.* Austin: Texas Parks & Wildlife Department.

Powell, A. Michael. 1988. *Trees and shrubs of Trans-Pecos Texas.* Big Bend National Park, Tex.: Big Bend Natural History Association.

Rasmussen, H. N. 1995. *Terrestrial orchids: From seed to mycotrophic plant.* Cambridge, Mass.: Cambridge University Press.

Reed, C. F. 1981. *Cypripedium kentuckiense* Reed, a new species of orchid in Kentucky. *Phytologia* 48: 426–428.

Riskind, David H., and David D. Diamond. 1988. An introduction to environments and vegetation. In *Edwards Plateau vegetation,* edited by Bonnie B. Amos and Frederick R. Gehlbach, 1–15. Waco, Tex.: Baylor University Press.

Salazar, Gerardo A. 1993. *Malaxis wendtii,* a new orchid species from Coahuila and Nuevo Leon, Mexico. *Orquidea* (Mexico) 13 (1–2): 281–284.

Sanders, Rogers W. 1997. Vegetation of Lennox Woods Preserve, Red River County, TX. *Texas Restoration Notes, Texas Society of Ecological Restoration* 2 (1).

Sheehan, Tom, and Marion Sheehan. 1994. *An illustrated survey of orchid genera.* Portland: Oregon Timber Press.

———. 1995. Orchid genera illustrated: 165: *Zeuxine.* American Orchid Society Bulletin 64 (7) 756–757.

Sheviak, Charles J. 1982. Biosystematic study of the *Spiranthes cernua* complex. Bulletin no. 448. Albany: New York State Museum.

———. 1995. *Cypripedium parviflorum* Salisb. I: The large-flowered plants and patterns of variation. *American Orchid Society Bulletin* 64: 606–612.

———. 1994. *Cypripedium parviflorum* Salisb. I: The small-flowered varieties. *American Orchid Society Bulletin* 63: 664–669.

———. 1974. *An introduction to the ecology of the Illinois Orchidaceae.* Springfield: Illinois State Museum.

———. 1991. Morphological variation in the compilospecies *Spiranthes cernua* (L.) L. C. Rich.: Ecologically-limited effects on gene flow. *Lindleyana* 6 (4): 228–234.

———. 1973. A new *Spiranthes* from the grasslands of central North America. Harvard University Botanical Museum Leaflets 23 (7).

———. 1983. United States terrestrial orchids—patterns and problems. In *Proceedings from Symposium II & Lectures: North American Terrestrial Orchids,* edited by Elmer H. Plaxton, 49–60. Livonia, Mich.: Michigan Orchid Society.

Singhurst, Jason R. 1996. The status of nine endangered plants of East Texas: Historical, ecological, and phytogeographic notes. Master's thesis, Stephen F. Austin State University.

Small, J. K. 1903. *Flora of the southeastern United States.* New York: Science Press.

Smith, Welby R. 1993. *Orchids of Minnesota.* Minneapolis: University of Minnesota Press.

Stewart, Joyce, H. P. Linder, E. A. Schelpe, and A. V. Hall. 1982. *Wild orchids of southern Africa.* Johannesburg: Macmillan South Africa.

Stones, Margaret, and Lowell Urbatsch. 1991. *Flora of Louisiana.* Baton Rouge and London: Louisiana State University Press.

Summers, Bill. 1987. *Missouri orchids.* Missouri Department of Conservation Natural History Series, no. 1.

Todsen, Thomas. 1995. *Malaxis wendtii* (Orchidaceae) in the United States. *Sida* 16 (3): 591.

Ward, J. R., and E. R. Nixon. 1992. Woody vegetation of the dry sandy uplands of eastern Texas. *Texas Journal of Science* 44: 283–294.

Warnock, Barton H. 1970. *Wildflowers of the Big Bend Country, Texas.* Alpine, Tex.: Sul Ross State University.

———. 1977. *Wildflowers of the Davis Mountains and the Marathon Basin, Texas.* Alpine, Tex.: Sul Ross State University.

Watson, Geraldine. 1979. *Big Thicket plant ecology: An introduction.* 2d ed. Saratoga, Tex.: Big Thicket Museum.

Whitlow, Carson E. 1983. *Cypripedium* culture. In *Proceedings from Symposium II & Lectures: North American Terrestrial Orchids,* edited by Elmer H. Plaxton, 25–31. Livonia, Mich.: Michigan Orchid Society.

Williams, John G., and Andrew E. Williams. 1983. *Field guide to orchids of North America.* New York: Universe Books.

## WORKS CONSULTED AND SELECTED BIBLIOGRAPHY FOR FURTHER READING

### GENERAL ORCHID BOOKS FOR THE LAYMAN

Bechtel, Helmut, Phillip Cribb, and Edmund Launert. 1986. *The manual of cultivated orchid species.* 2d ed. Cambridge, Mass.: The MIT Press.

Bernhardt, Peter. 1989. *Wily violets and underground orchids: Revelations of a botanist.* New York: William Morrow.

Kramer, Jack. 1989. *The World Wildlife Fund book of orchids.* 2d ed. New York: Abbeville Press.

Shuttleworth, Floyd S., Herbert S. Zim, and Gordon Dillon. 1970. *Orchids.* New York: Golden Press.

Squire, David. 1992. *The little book of orchids.* New York: Mallard Press.

### REGIONAL ORCHID REFERENCES

Cady, Leo, and E. R. Rotherham. 1970. *Australian native orchids in color.* Rutland, Vt.: Charles E. Tuttle.

Coleman, Ronald A. 1995. *The wild orchids of California.* Ithaca, N.Y.: Cornell University Press.

Davies, Paul, Jenne Davies, and Anthony Huxley. 1983. *Wild orchids of Britain and Europe.* London: Chato & Windus—The Hogarth Press.

Gibson, William H. 1905. *Our native orchids.* New York: Doubleday, Page.

Gupton, Oxcar W., and Fred C. Swope. 1986. *Wild orchids of the Middle Atlantic States.* Knoxville: The University of Tennessee Press.

Petrie, Dr. W. 1981. *Guide to orchids of North America.* Vancouver, Canada: Hancock House Publishers.

Slaughter, Carl R. 1993. *Wild orchids of Arkansas.* Petit Jean Mountain, Ark.: Carl R. Slaughter, M.D. Self-published.

Smith, Welby R. 1993. *Orchids of Minnesota.* Minneapolis: University of Minnesota Press.

Summers, Bill. 1987. *Missouri orchids.* Missouri Department of Conservation Natural History Series, no. 1.

Wiard, Leon A. 1987. *An introduction to the orchids of Mexico.* Ithaca, N.Y.: Comstock Publishing Associates, Cornell University.

Williams, John G., Andrew E. Williams, and Norman Arlott. 1978. *Field guide to orchids of Britain and Europe with North Africa and the Middle East.* London: William Collins.

### BOOKS

Doughty, Robin, and Barbara M. Parmenter. 1989. *Endangered species: Disappearing animals and plants in the Lone Star State.* Austin: Texas Monthly Press.

Gledhill, D. 1989. *The names of plants.* 2d ed. Cambridge: Cambridge University Press.

Imes, Rick. 1990. *The practical botanist.* New York: Simon & Schuster.

Loughmiller, Campbell, and Lynn Loughmiller. 1984. *Texas wildflowers.* Austin: University of Texas Press.

Moldenke, Harold N. 1949. *American wild flowers.* New York, Toronto, and London: D. Van Nostrand Company.

Parks, H. B., et al. 1936. *Biological survey of the East Texas Big Thicket Area.* Sponsored by Texas Academy of Science.

Rickett, Harold William. 1969. *Wildflowers of the United States, volume 3: Texas.* New York: McGraw-Hill.

Watson, Geraldine. 1982. *Vegetational survey of Big Thicket National Preserve.* Washington, D.C.: National Park Service.

Weniger, Del. 1984. *The explorers' Texas: The lands and waters.* Austin, Tex.: Eakin Publications.

### ARTICLES

Anderson, Allan B. 1991. Symbiotic and asymbiotic germination and growth of *Spiranthes magnicamporum* (Orchidaceae). *Lindleyana* 6 (4): 183–186.

Clements, Mark A. 1988. Orchid mycorrhizal associations. *Lindleyana* 3 (2): 73–86.

Currah, R. S. 1991. Taxonomic and developmental aspects of the fungal endophytes of terrestrial orchid mycorrhizae. *Lindleyana* 6 (4): 211–213.

Folkerts, George W. 1982. The Gulf Coast pitcher plant bogs. *American Scientist* 70: 260–267.

Hagan, Patti. 1991. Gardening: Save the wildflowers. *Wall Street Journal* (November 19): A12.

Marden, Luis. 1971. The exquisite orchids. *National Geographic* 139, no. 4 (April): 485–513.

Pridgeon, Alec M., and Lowell E. Urbatsch. 1977. Contributions to the flora of Louisiana II: Distribution and identification of the orchidaceae. *Castanea* 42: 293–304.

# Index

Page numbers in **boldface** indicate species descriptions; *Italic* numbers indicate photographs.